Strategies for Hypergrowth

Roger Cartwright

T0341696

STRATEGY

03.05

- ■ Fast track route to mastering and managing rapid growth

- ■ Covers the key drivers of hypergrowth, from focussing intensely on customers and constant innovation to ensuring resources are in place and making sure you stay on track

- ■ Examples and lessons from benchmark companies, including Cisco, Nike, Samsung and Airbus Industrie, and ideas from the smartest thinkers including Patricia Anslinger, Thomas Copeland, David Korten, Michael Porter and Noel M. Tichy

- ■ Includes a glossary of key concepts and a comprehensive resources guide

>>EXPRESS EXEC.COM<<
essential management thinking at your fingertips

First published 2002 by
Capstone Publishing (a Wiley company)
8 Newtec Place
Magdalen Road
Oxford OX4 1RE
United Kingdom
http://www.capstoneideas.com

CIP catalogue records for this book are available from the British Library and the US Library of Congress

ISBN 1-84112-210-6

This book is printed on acid-free paper

Substantial discounts on bulk quantities of Capstone books are available to corporations, professional associations and other organizations. Please contact Capstone for more details on +44 (0)1865 798 623 or (fax) +44 (0)1865 240 941 or (e-mail) info@wiley-capstone.co.uk

Contents

Introduction to ExpressExec

ExpressExec is 3 million words of the latest management thinking compiled into 10 modules. Each module contains 10 individual titles forming a comprehensive resource of current business practice written by leading practitioners in their field. From brand management to balanced scorecard, ExpressExec enables you to grasp the key concepts behind each subject and implement the theory immediately. Each of the 100 titles is available in print and electronic formats.

Through the ExpressExec.com Website you will discover that you can access the complete resource in a number of ways:

» printed books or e-books;
» e-content – PDF or XML (for licensed syndication) adding value to an intranet or Internet site;
» a corporate e-learning/knowledge management solution providing a cost-effective platform for developing skills and sharing knowledge within an organization;
» bespoke delivery – tailored solutions to solve your need.

Why not visit www.expressexec.com and register for free key management briefings, a monthly newsletter and interactive skills checklists. Share your ideas about ExpressExec and your thoughts about business today.

Please contact elound@wiley-capstone.co.uk for more information.

Introduction to Hypergrowth Strategies

This chapter considers how hypergrowth:

- » is the rapid expansion of an organization;
- » is not restricted to the private, commercial sector but can be seen in governmental and voluntary organizations;
- » can be ephemeral;
- » often occurs at times of rapid technological change;
- » has been a feature of organizational life since the eighteenth century.

Hypergrowth refers to the phenomenon of the exceedingly rapid expansion of an organization. The organization is usually a private company but the public sector can also experience hypergrowth. The Manhattan Project that led to the US and the UK developing the first nuclear weapons between 1942 and 1945 was an example of a government-sponsored operation that grew exceedingly quickly, possibly quicker than any other official project had before it.

Hypergrowth is not always successful, sustained growth. It is possible for organizations to grow so quickly that they run out of the vital resources needed to nourish and sustain their operations. This will be referred to in this material but the concentration will be on strategies for success.

Like living things, organizations need certain external factors to grow, the most important of which are a source of nutrients (raw, materials, money, skills etc.) and a secure environment. As hypergrowth consumes vast amounts of external resource it is a phenomenon usually shown by large organizations as only they are able to accumulate resources in the huge amounts necessary.

It is not unusual in nature for organisms to be ephemeral – for example those plants that have lain dormant in arid areas and then spring up and grow rapidly after rain, flowering in a very short period of time and then dying back. Other types of plants, the Russian vine and the Kudzu in the southern states of the US put on regular spectacular growth. Companies can be the same. The last years of the twentieth century saw a profusion of dot com companies springing up, with many dying away almost as fast as they came. The decline of businesses is nothing new, the commercial world is dynamic and new companies start up with some surviving much longer through the organizational life cycle than others. What was noticeable about the dot-com revolution was the rapid increase in the quoted worth of the companies before they made any profit at all – a point covered in more detail in Chapter 3. The experience of the dot-com companies was not a new one; the rapid increase in share price without any trade revenue to support it was a characteristic of the South Sea Bubble Scandal in the UK in the eighteenth century and railway mania also in the UK, with the collapse of Charles Hudson's empire a century later in 1847. What links the South Sea Bubble, the railway mania and the dot-com companies is that they all came to prominence at a time of intense technological and communication growth that sparked considerable public interest. Those that survived in earlier times and those dot com companies that look likely to continue with their growth are those that have realized that changing the medium of trade does not absolve the company of the existing rules of business, not least of which are listening to the customer, delivering quality and looking after the financial side of the operation.

Companies that experience hypergrowth need to control it or else it becomes like a conflagration that dies away because it has burnt up all the oxygen. The examples in this material – Nike, Cisco Systems, Carnival Group, Airbus Industrie, and Samsung – are companies that have managed to grow rapidly but in a manner that means they have not outstripped their resources. Their growth has not been smooth but it has been spectacular. They are very different companies but they have in common the fact that they have shown that hypergrowth can be managed by those who understand that growing too quickly can be as dangerous and destructive as either growing too slowly or not growing at all.

What Is Meant by Hypergrowth?

This chapter examines the following concepts relating to hypergrowth:

» Hypergrowth occurs when an organization is growing at a much faster rate than other similar organizations.
» Hypergrowth may be successful or unsuccessful. The latter often leads to the demise of the organization.
» A rapidly increasing market share is an indicator of hypergrowth.
» Cashflow and the input of resources need very careful control during a period of hypergrowth.
» Hypergrowth organizations are most likely to be found at the adolescence stage of the organizational life cycle.
» The adolescence stage is also when companies are most vulnerable to takeovers.
» A succession of high market share in a growing market (*stars*) are a feature of successful hypergrowth companies.
» Governments etc. may step in to limit hypergrowth if they feel that the stability of the market is threatened or that a monopoly is developing.

HYPERGROWTH – DEFINITION OF

H. Skip Weitzen in his book, *Hypergrowth - Applying the Success Formula of Today's Fastest Growing Companies* (1991) defined hypergrowth as occurring when a company generates $1bn or more of sales within a decade of incorporation or emergence from a dormant position.

Under this definition, Weitzen believes that hypergrowth is a phenomenon first encountered in the 1980s in the US and that it has continued throughout the 1990s and into the twenty-first century.

It is the contention of the writer of this material that hypergrowth cannot be defined in absolute terms but is more relative in nature. Hypergrowth can be said to occur when a company (or even a public service) grows at a much faster rate than similar organizations in the same market. Indeed it is possible for a market itself to undergo hypergrowth with a number of companies all growing at a spectacular rate.

THE IMPORTANCE OF MARKET SHARE

As an indicator of hypergrowth, market share is more revealing than just using financial and raw sales data. As stated above, it may well be that all of the major players in a market are growing. The reasons for this may be less to do with what the individual organization is doing and more to do with a sudden upsurge in demand. In the late 1940s and early 1950, both the US and the UK automobile manufacturers experienced a degree of hypergrowth. This was more connected to the lifting of wartime restrictions, increases in disposable income and the availability of product than the actual quality of the various models. Customers were so desperate to buy that it would have been difficult for an automobile manufacturer not to exhibit hypergrowth.

If, however, one or two of the players are also increasing their market share this indicates that they are being more successful than the others are – it is they that are in or approaching hypergrowth.

SUCCESSFUL AND UNSUCCESSFUL HYPERGROWTH

In 1966, the Douglas Aircraft Corporation of California had firm orders for 409 of its twin-engined DC9 airliners plus options for another 104 placed by its airline customers. This was in addition to 138 firm orders and 40 options for the established four-engined DC10. The Vietnam War was raging and as a supplier of fighter-bombers to the United States Air Force (USAF) and Navy (USN), Douglas was definitely in hypergrowth.

In November 1966, as reported by Paul Eddy and his colleagues (1976), Stanley de Jongh Osborne of the investment firm of Lazard Freres had the unenviable task of telling the Douglas board that the company was bankrupt.

One can only empathize with the feelings of the Douglas board – full order books and yet they were bankrupt. What had happened is a classic example of unsuccessful hypergrowth. Three factors brought Douglas to this position:

1 They ran out of cash. Cashflow is an exceptionally important concept in business. For a company such as Douglas with a great deal of its balance sheet assets in the form of buildings, plant, inventory etc. it is important that there is actually enough cash available to pay the bills. There is no point in owning a $5mn house if you do not have enough money in your pocket to pay the clerk at the supermarket for $50 worth of groceries. They will be uninterested in your longer-term assets; they just want $50 in cash. It would be a shame if you had to sell your house to raise the $50! Douglas owed money to its suppliers and its banks and they wanted their money.

2 Costs were not being controlled. Companies make a profit when sales revenue exceeds costs and overheads. To fulfill their orders Douglas had taken on a large number of new hires and their lack of experience meant that it was taking far longer to complete an aircraft than it should have done. Thus each aircraft was costing more than anticipated to build – often more than the price being charged to the customer. A recipe for disaster.

3 Inventory control was poor. The building time was further aggravated by the fact that the Vietnam War was putting a huge strain on the supply of resources for the aviation industry. Building a modern aircraft means that components must arrive at the assembly plant on a JIT (just in time) basis. This was not happening, and part completed aircraft were left waiting for vital components. This tied up the assembly lines and left the aircraft unpaid for.

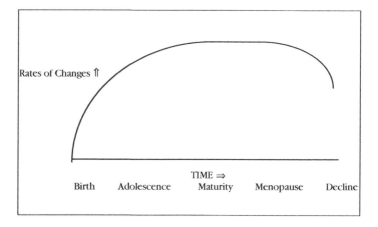

Fig. 2.1

For hypergrowth to be successful cashflow, costs and inventory/supplies must be controlled. It is easy for these areas to be neglected in the euphoria of gaining orders. If they are neglected, however, the case above shows that even an organization with a healthy order book can be brought down unless careful controls are in place.

THE LIFE CYCLE OF ORGANIZATIONS

Organizations undergo a life cycle similar to that for products and indeed similar to that for human beings. Marketing experts use a concept called the product life cycle and Roger Cartwright and George Green (1997) adapted this idea when they put forward the concept of an organizational life cycle (see Fig. 2.1). They suggested that organizations, like products, go through a series of changes:

» birth
» adolescence
» maturity
» menopause
» decline.

They suggested that it was possible for changes at the menopausal stage to result in decline being averted and the organization gaining a new, albeit different, lease of life. There is a more detailed discussion of the whole organizational life cycle in *Managing Growth* – a companion volume in the *ExpressExec* series.

In the context of hypergrowth it is often the adolescent organization that benefits.

Provided that an organization survives its birth process, by adolescence it should be gaining in both confidence and sophistication and is likely to be fairly entrepreneurial. As William Heinecke and Jonathon Marsh wrote in 2000, the entrepreneurial culture should be fun, and adolescent organizations are renowned for both their dynamism and the sense of enjoyment (and occasional frustration) enjoyed by those associated with them. Dynamism is something closely associated with hypergrowth and it is not surprising that hypergrowth is often linked with entrepreneurial figures.

Adolescence can be a very vulnerable time for an organization, especially one in hypergrowth as it may be vulnerable to takeover by more established players seeking to benefit from its hypergrowth. Adolescent organizations often have cashflow problems associated with growth and a cash rich competitor may attempt to gain control or use the cash situation to force the organization out of the market. The acquisition of the highly successful but relatively young Princess Cruises (of Love Boat® television series fame) by the much older UK-based P&O Group in 1974 was a classic example of this. Princess Cruises was growing fast but P&O wanted a presence in the US market. Under P&O management the Princess operation has flourished and has a very healthy position in the market but not as high as the Carnival brand detailed in Chapter 7.

Where an organization is in hypergrowth the period of adolescence appears to last much longer than for others. The dynamism does die away.

PROLONGING ADOLESCENCE AND COMPARTMENTALIZED HYPERGROWTH

It was mentioned earlier that many hypergrowth operations are linked to entrepreneurial figures. Individual vision, drive and commitment are an important factor in developing and sustaining hypergrowth. If you have started your own business or are very senior in an established concern you will need to ensure that the vision you have and your wish to achieve hypergrowth is communicated to all involved in the functioning of the organization.

In the Boston Matrix used to describe product portfolios, a product for which a company has a high market share in a growing market is known as a *star*. Hypergrowth companies need a succession of *stars*. As the market growth slows, provided the company still has a healthy market share the product becomes a *cash cow*. All of the development work has been paid for and while profits are normally not spectacular from such products they are steady and reliable.

Companies in hypergrowth are characterized by having a succession of *stars*. Microsoft is continually bringing out new software. They use what may be the ultimate hypergrowth strategy – make your product out of date and sell the customer a replacement. The life cycle for some products is very long, for others it is very short. The cases in this book contain examples of products with very long life cycles – a Carnival cruise ship will probably spend ten or so years with the company before being sold. Airlines hold on to their Airbus A320s for many years. A camcorder on the other hand may be replaced by a more up-to-date model after just a few years while a Nike shoe might be replaced by the latest style next year.

The strategy that hypergrowth companies employ is to always have the next *star* on the way before the current one enters decline. In this way adolescence and its dynamism can be prolonged.

MUST GROWTH STOP?

All systems cease to grow when the supply of resources into them declines or external factors limit growth. As was shown in the Douglas example earlier, unless the resources can be brought in and applied correctly there may still be apparent growth but the organization is actually in decline – a decline that becomes very rapid as people begin to see what is really happening.

Organization both in the private and public sectors may have legislative constraints put on their growth. Concerns that Microsoft was becoming too large and powerful prompted legal action against the company by the US government. By 2001 the matter had still not been settled: a ruling that Microsoft should be divided into two separate concerns having been overruled and the issue was back before the courts.

KEY LEARNING POINTS

» Hypergrowth may be successful or unsuccessful.
» Uncontrolled hypergrowth may destroy the organization.
» Sales alone cannot provide a complete definition of hypergrowth. The position of the organization relative to others is also an important factor.
» Hypergrowth is most often seen in adolescent organizations and it is also a time of vulnerability.
» Hypergrowth requires a succession of *stars*.
» If too much hypergrowth occurs the outside environment (often in the form of government action) may step in to place limits on growth.

The Evolution of Hypergrowth

This chapter examines how hypergrowth has evolved. It explains how:

» Hypergrowth began with new ways of financing ventures in the eighteenth century as more and more of the general population in developed countries had an opportunity to invest.

» The Industrial Revolution brought about a transformation in both communication and the size of organizations laying the foundations for even greater hypergrowth.

» Henceforth growth occurred in industry rather than as a result of land ownership.

» Both world wars, devastating as they were, gave companies opportunities to expand and brought forth technological developments.

» Since 1945 the ICT, finance and leisure sectors have experienced hypergrowth.

» Growth in dot-com companies was initially very rapid but many investors pulled out as it became apparent that quick returns were not to be had.

As stated in the last chapter, H. Skip Weitzen in his book, *Hypergrowth – Applying the Success Formula of Today's Fastest Growing Companies* (1991) defined hypergrowth as occurring when a company generates $1bn or more of sales within a decade of incorporation or emergence from a dormant position.

Under this definition, Weitzen believes that hypergrowth is a phenomenon first encountered in the 1980s in the US and that it has continued throughout the 1990s and into the twenty-first century.

If the concept of hypergrowth as being a relative rather than an absolute concept is considered, then hypergrowth was first recorded as early as the start of the eighteenth century.

FINANCING OPERATIONS

Early business ventures were in the main either small-scale family businesses or single trading ventures.

Many of the early trading ventures were linked to the voyages of discovery that set out from Europe from the fifteenth century onwards. These voyages were a partnership between the explorer and those who risked not their lives but their capital on a successful venture. The financiers of the early ventures were often the rulers of the country but soon merchants began to invest in them. While the original ventures tended to be single projects with cargo and ship being sold off upon return to harbor, soon organizations as we know them today began to develop – organizations that had an existence that lasted longer than a single venture. While family firms had this form of structure, larger projects had tended to be "one-off." Such project operations still occur today. The forming of TML (Trans Manche Link) to build the Channel Tunnel between the UK and France in the 1980s–90s is an example – the organization being formed as a consortium of engineering companies for a single task.

An investor with money could share vicariously in the excitement of the exploration age by putting money into a trading venture and with luck would make a profit. These ventures were not like the incorporated or joint stock companies of today. At the end of each venture the syndicate would divide all of the profits and dissolve. This was a very inefficient method of managing increasing large commercial ventures and thus companies, far larger than the family businesses then engaged in manufacturing or trade, were set up to exist beyond a particular venture. Many of these companies sought investment not just from wealthy private benefactors but also from a growing middle class – made prosperous by the very growth in trade it was now to help finance. Unfortunately, the early stock market was just as volatile then as it is today and after the South Sea Bubble fiasco of 1720 (see later) the British government began to regulate trade and its financial aspects more rigorously.

The South Sea Bubble plan – the first of the huge public offerings of stock in a privately owned venture – was devised by Robert Harley, the Earl of Oxford, in 1711, for paying off Great Britain's national debt. Under the plan, the debt was assumed by merchants to whom the government guaranteed for a certain period annual payments equal to $3mn. This sum, amounting to 6 percent interest, was to be obtained from duties on imports from certain areas, namely the Pacific Ocean trade that was just beginning to be developed. The monopoly held by sections of British trade in the South Seas and South America was given to these merchants, incorporated as the South Sea Company, and extravagant ideas of the riches of South America and the South Seas were fostered to attract investors. This early example of hype was the first but not the last time attempts were made to raise capital by presenting a rosier picture than was actually the case. In the spring of 1720 the company offered to assume practically the whole national debt, at that time equal to more than $150mn. Companies of all kinds were floated to take advantage of the public interest in obtaining South Sea Company stock. Speculation soon carried stock to ten times its nominal value despite there being no actual earnings at the time. The chairman and some directors sold out, the bubble burst, and the stock collapsed. Thousands of stockholders were ruined. Parliamentary investigation revealed complicity by some company officials and other public notables including members of the royal court of George I. However, a political crisis was averted through the efforts of Sir Robert Walpole, who at that time was serving as the Chancellor of the Exchequer and later became the first person to hold a post equated with that of the present day UK Prime Minister. Only about one-third of the original capital was recovered for the stockholders.

Despite this failure the public soon took to this form of investment and companies were able to raise money through ownership rather than borrowing. This greatly aided those with new ideas and who could convince investors to take a modest risk with them. Investors by their weight of numbers were spreading individual risk and thus facilitating the growth of companies. In areas where a large return was anticipated the prospects for hypergrowth became very real.

HYPERGROWTH AND THE INDUSTRIAL REVOLUTION

Beginning predominantly in the UK, the Industrial Revolution started with the application of steam power to industry in the late eighteenth century. As soon as steam began to be used for communication, both the Liverpool and Manchester Railway in the UK and the Baltimore and Ohio Railway in the US began regular steam operations for both passengers and freight in 1830, the stage was set for hypergrowth in manufacturing.

The railways enabled workers to live further from their employment, thus increasing the physical size of companies, and meant that larger components could be swiftly and easily transported from site to site. At the same time steam power was being applied to the shipping industry and iron (and later steel) was replacing wood as the principal raw material used to build ships.

Examples from both the railroad and the shipping industries show how hypergrowth occurred in them.

The Baltimore and Ohio Railroad cost $4mn to build in 1830; 75 percent of this sum came from individual investors with virtually no Federal assistance at all. As a matter of interest, Chicago in 1830 had a population of just 100! By 1867 Canada had a total of 2459 miles of railroad built at a cost of US$155mn of which 20 percent was government funding.

In 1865 at the end of the Civil War there were 35,000 miles of track in use in the US, by 1888 this number had increased by a factor of over 4 to 156,000. The national expansion of large organizations was now possible. The railroads themselves together with the shipping companies that were moving increasing numbers of emigrants across the Atlantic were among the largest of these new industrial giants as were the iron and steel works, mining, engineering and chemical plants that were being developed at an increasing rate.

In the UK, the City of Manchester (original terminus of the Liverpool and Manchester Railway) had a population of 50,000 in 1775. Due to the increase in industrial activity, the combined population of Manchester and Salford (the city on the other side of the River Irwell) had increased eightfold by 1830 when the Liverpool and Manchester Railway commenced commercial operations, and had doubled again by 1850. Half of the funding for the Liverpool and Manchester Railway came from Liverpool interests, particularly in the cotton industry. The area around Manchester is noted for its fresh water and abundant rainfall – the right environment for spinning cotton. It is no coincidence that the sympathies of the population of the northwest of England were with the Confederacy in the US Civil War. They were so strong in fact that many in the Confederate hierarchy believed that Britain might enter the war on their side; so important was the cotton trade to UK prosperity. By 1850 the home industries relying on a simple loom had been replaced by huge mills employing many hundreds of people, often in very poor conditions.

Those who invested in the railways had the chance to make considerable fortunes before the railway bubble burst. In the UK this happened fairly early with the "railway mania" of the late 1840s. When the bubble burst, those who had invested in the schemes of the so-called "Railway King," George Hudson, lost heavily. However, those who had invested in the major companies, such as the Great Western, the Midland etc., saw them grow to cover whole regions of the country. A similar pattern occurred in the US where Vanderbilt and Morgan made their initial millions on railroad-related investments.

These people, whose names have become synonymous with wealth, were unique in that they were among the first to make their money from manufacturing rather than from the ownership of land. While in Europe many of the landed gentry eschewed trade and manufacturing, in the US it was a different story. A secondary "trade" soon grew involving the marriage of the daughters of UK aristocracy to the US manufacturing barons and their sons!

On the seas, the size of ships was increasing so that the largest ship in 1900, White Star's of 17,272 GRT (gross registered tonnage – a measure of volume not weight), was less than half the size of their *Olympic* (45,324) launched only 11 years later. Not only was there hypergrowth in the shipping lines but also in the steel mills and shipyards that provided the material and the vessels. By acquiring White Star as part of his International Mercantile Marine empire, J P Morgan also gained access to their builder, Harland and Wolff and set out to build the largest shipping operation ever seen – an ambition thwarted by the outbreak of war in Europe in 1914.

DREADNOUGHT

The proof that hypergrowth had occurred within the shipbuilding industry was dramatically evidenced in 1906. By 1905 the Royal Navy operated no fewer than 45 battleships in commission, enough to meet the policy of matching the combined strength of the next two largest navies. In 1906 the First Sea Lord, Admiral "Jackie" Fisher threw the advantage away and put all the world's navies on a level playing field.

In great secrecy and completed in a record 366 days, HMS *Dreadnought* rendered every other battleship (including those of the Royal Navy) obsolete overnight. Previous battleships had been equipped with reciprocating engines and four large guns. *Dreadnought* employed the revolutionary steam turbine developed by Charles Parsons to increase her speed by 3–4 knots and a battery of no fewer than ten 12-inch guns. The new engines weighed less allowing for more armor to be worked into the hull and did not suffer from vibration. Twelve-inch guns were not the largest afloat – earlier Royal Navy ships had mounted 13.5-inch guns but no ship that fast had carried ten big guns.

The Royal Navy might not have been the first to introduce the Dreadnought concept. The US Navy, the Japanese and the Italians had been working towards it. The UK was the only country that could make its existing fleet obsolete, however, safe in the knowledge that the hypergrowth in its shipbuilding industry gave it the resources to regain its supremacy with alacrity.

That it succeeded is shown by the fact that by 1918 the following Dreadnought-type battleships had been laid down:

» UK: 51
» Germany: 27 (1 sold to Turkey)

» US: 16
» Japan: 10 (1 built in the UK)
» France: 7
» Italy: 6
» Austria: 4
» Brazil: 2 (built in UK yards).

No other country could have achieved that rate of building. In fact the vast majority were completed before the outbreak of hostilities in 1914. In addition there were numerous merchant ships including six large transatlantic liners completed in UK yards at the same time.

FIRST WORLD WAR

In terms of business the years 1914–18 saw the emergence of the US as the main economic power in the world. While the US did not enter the war until 1917, US industries had been expanding at a phenomenal rate to meet the orders placed by the UK and France. All sectors benefited, from agriculture to manufacturing.

For the first time in the developed world, whole economies were mobilized in the national interest and production line techniques were honed together with rapid advances in the technologies of chemicals (important for explosives), medicine, communication and aviation.

After the war it was not long before the world entered a deep economic recession that did not lift until, paradoxically, the flames of war were relit. Again the US was the main beneficiary. American industry supported the UK through the dark days of 1940 and 1941 and when the US entered the war late in 1941 the full might of US commerce was as important to victory as military prowess. Production line methods, honed by the war, became the norm and organizations tended to become larger and larger, even though the economic conditions were against economic hypergrowth. In the public sector, however, both the US and Germany undertook a huge growth in public work programs to help relieve unemployment. Full employment was to come soon enough as the world was plunged into yet another global conflict.

1939–45

While the US military did not enter the war (formally) until December 1941 (the Royal Air Force aircraft that found the German battleship *Bismarck* in May 1941 was piloted by Ensign Leonard B. Smith, United States Navy), US industry had been engaged on war work since September 1939. The war effort of the allied nations probably represents the greatest degree of hypergrowth ever seen. From its first delivery in 1939 until April 1945 over 12,000 Boeing B-17 Flying Fortress bombers were delivered in addition to over 3000 of its successor, the huge B-29 Flying Fortress. Tanks, Jeeps, liberty ships, artillery, engines for vehicles and planes – the factories of the US and the UK were as much a part of the war effort as those on the front line. Whole new design and manufacturing methods were developed culminating in the Manhattan Project to develop the atomic bomb.

POST-WAR

When the war ended the industries of Europe and Japan might have been devastated but those of the US were at the peak of their production.

The war had also provided an impetus for scientific developments especially in what is now known as ICT (information and communication technology). This, financial services and leisure were to be the hypergrowth areas of the rest of the twentieth century and into the twenty-first.

Computers and telephone technology was to dominate firstly business operations and then the home. Television moved from primitive black and white sets in the 1950s to the color sets of today in a relatively short period of time. Messages were relayed not along wires but via satellites in space. This increase in communication allowed money to flow ever faster around the world. People in the developed world had more leisure time and relatively higher earnings leading to hypergrowth in the vacation, leisure and entertainment industries – much of which is still continuing as shown by the Carnival Group case study in Chapter 7.

By the end of the 1980s companies such as Compaq, Reebok, Wal-Mart and Federal Express had broken the "$1bn in a decade" mark set by Weitzen and hypergrowth seems set to be a phenomenon of the twenty-first century for those companies that have the strategies to exploit opportunities and maintain growth.

THE DOT-COM HYPERGROWTH

The development of the Internet in the 1990s and its rapid acceptance as a means of communication, information gathering and trade by the millennium led to hypergrowth in a new type of company that traded only via the Internet – the dot-com company, named after the Internet suffix that such companies were allocated.

The latter part of the 1990s saw a phenomenal growth in both the number of such companies and the willingness of investors to fund them – a bubble that began to burst almost as soon as it began. The analysts who were predicting easy gains for investors in dot-com operations had apparently neglected to consider the customer. While investment grew, customer numbers did not grow at nearly the rate necessary for the survival of many of the operations.

The case of GovWorks.com founded in the US in 1998 by Kaleil Isaza Tuzman and Tom Herman serves to illustrate the point. The concept was a good one. People would be able to deal with official agencies and purchase licenses or pay parking fines etc. over the Internet, irrespective of office opening hours. New York City and the Commonwealth of Massachusetts were among GovWorks.com's clients but the customer base never became large enough, and in 2001 the company filed for bankruptcy having used up over $65mn in start-up funding and reached a peak of 250 employees. Perhaps later on the idea will resurface and be successful. The acceptability of the Internet as a trading medium has, unfortunately, been slower to grow among customers than it has with those who offer the services.

Amazon.com has been one of the most successful of the early dot-com companies. Initially specializing in books and later in music, Jeff Bezos, the founder of Amazon, chose a product (books) that was already well known and possessed a large, mature market. All he really did was change the means of making the transaction between vendor and customer. From its launch in 1995 Amazon now operates not only in the US but also in the UK, Germany, France and Japan. Amazon's sales in 1999, just 4 years after start-up were $2.6bn, but the company had

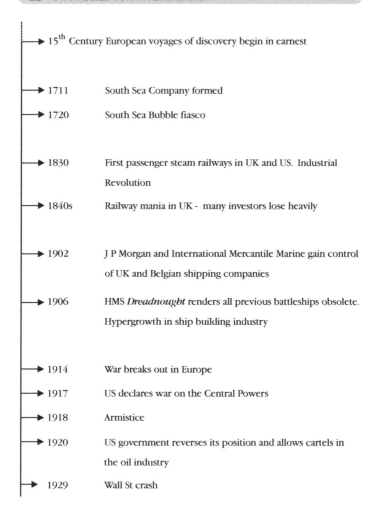

→ 15ᵗʰ Century European voyages of discovery begin in earnest

→ 1711 South Sea Company formed

→ 1720 South Sea Bubble fiasco

→ 1830 First passenger steam railways in UK and US. Industrial Revolution

→ 1840s Railway mania in UK - many investors lose heavily

→ 1902 J P Morgan and International Mercantile Marine gain control of UK and Belgian shipping companies

→ 1906 HMS *Dreadnought* renders all previous battleships obsolete. Hypergrowth in ship building industry

→ 1914 War breaks out in Europe

→ 1917 US declares war on the Central Powers

→ 1918 Armistice

→ 1920 US government reverses its position and allows cartels in the oil industry

→ 1929 Wall St crash

Fig. 3.1

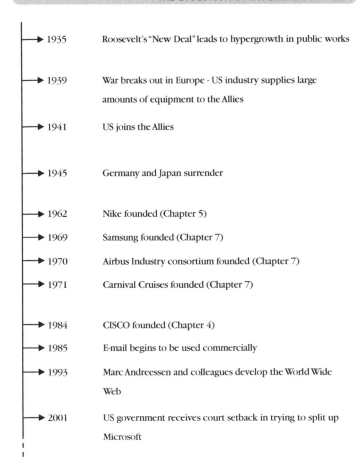

1935	Roosevelt's "New Deal" leads to hypergrowth in public works
1939	War breaks out in Europe - US industry supplies large amounts of equipment to the Allies
1941	US joins the Allies
1945	Germany and Japan surrender
1962	Nike founded (Chapter 5)
1969	Samsung founded (Chapter 7)
1970	Airbus Industry consortium founded (Chapter 7)
1971	Carnival Cruises founded (Chapter 7)
1984	CISCO founded (Chapter 4)
1985	E-mail begins to be used commercially
1993	Marc Andreessen and colleagues develop the World Wide Web
2001	US government receives court setback in trying to split up Microsoft

Fig. 3.1   *(Continued).*

not gone into profit and was still making losses. The costs of running such an organization have proved to be large. Amazon is fortunate in that its investors have continued to see the potential and have mainly kept their money in the company. Many other dot-coms have not been so fortunate and have seen investors bailing out as anticipated profits have been replaced with continuing losses. It is perhaps unfortunate that the dot-com revolution occurred at a time when Western investors were taking ever shorter-term views and demanding quick returns on their investments.

It is interesting to note that the largest US companies see traditional competitors, not new entrants or "dot-coms," as the greatest threat to their successful e-business forays, according to a 2001 survey conducted by the consulting company PricewaterhouseCoopers (see Chapter 9).

The survey found that over 40 percent of the companies taking part indicated that traditional competitors with e-business capabilities pose the greatest threat, as e-business takes hold and begins to transform their companies. Only 13 percent identified dot-com companies, i.e. those companies that only operate via the Internet, as the greatest competitive threat.

A timeline for hypergrowth is shown as Fig. 3.1.

KEY LEARNING POINTS

» Hypergrowth is not a new phenomenon but it has never been seen at the current scale before.
» Different sectors of business can experience hypergrowth at different times.
» External factors such as wars can actually aid hypergrowth.

The E-Dimension

This chapter explores how:

» The development of the Internet has allowed all kinds of companies to expand their customer base.
» The vast majority of organizations whether in the private or public sector now have a presence on the Web.
» Suppliers of Internet-related products have been best placed to take advantage of the growth in the Internet and e-commerce. Some of these companies, e.g. Cisco, have experienced hypergrowth.
» There is still a reluctance among some consumers to purchase online.

The Internet has not been the cause of hypergrowth for companies in traditional commercial areas but it has enabled them to gather information and communicate much more effectively. Some companies, however, owe their existence and their phenomenal growth to Internet and connected computer developments and it is one of those, Cisco Systems, that features in the best practice section at the end of this chapter.

No organization can afford not to have a Web presence as this is where many potential customers now go in order to find out about the organization and its products. Online catalogs for everything from computers to gardening are available on the Internet with the advantage that they can be much more up to date than a printed version. More and more companies are including details of their commitments to the environment and the community on their Websites as well as virtual tours of facilities, as described in the case study on Nike in the next chapter. The Internet is rapidly becoming a major means of communication between organizations and their customers. More and more customers are also using it to communicate to the organization and as faith in payment systems grows, so more and more are using it to make purchases.

In the course of only about 18 months at the end of the twentieth and beginning of the twenty-first centuries virtually every UK bank moved into offering a home banking service, with take-up rates being very high.

Websites need to be maintained and updated and this has provided a huge growth area for companies in this field.

The suppliers of hardware also benefit from this growth. There are few offices in the world without a personal computer in them and in the developed world the same is true of homes.

In addition to the suppliers of hardware there are also growth opportunities for software developers (Microsoft is a global name that is almost as well known as Coca-Cola) and the suppliers of the essential but more mundane items – disks, cables, paper etc.

INTERNET-SPECIFIC COMPANIES

There are those companies that have grown as a direct result of the development of the Internet. The companies developing search engines have shown rapid growth (a number of them are profiled by Christopher Price in his book *The Internet Entrepreneurs*). Yahoo!, Lycos, AltaVista, Excite etc. are also global names and provide an essential link between that other growth area, the ISP (Internet Service Provider) – such as AOL, Supranet, Virgin Net, CompuServe, BTnet etc. – and the customer and the Web page. To be used properly the Internet needs all these components working in unison. While consumers pay for ISP services, search engines are funded through advertising.

Organizations seeking high growth rates will use any and every suitable medium and not concentrate on just one. Those organizations that have used the Internet effectively have discovered that their customer base can be expanded extremely rapidly and that growth is only limited by the physical logistics of delivering the product. If, as in the case of software or financial services, the product can actually be delivered over the net the only physical limit on hypergrowth is the actual number of terminals in the world.

The Internet has grown not only in size but also in sophistication. If one is thinking of buying a house, a virtual tour is a possibility. Vacations can be "tried" before purchase. The limits appear to be only those of the imagination.

Any system with huge numbers of links will assist hypergrowth by providing additional synergy between components. The more links there are, the more connections can be made and hypergrowth comes from connections.

Microsoft's hypergrowth stems from the connectivity between its operating system, its software and the Internet. Amazon.com has, in effect made every purchaser of a book from its site a branch of the organization. By feeding back preferences into the system, Amazon are able to offer increased added value on the next visit by suggesting items that the customer might enjoy. It is this synergy that makes the Internet such a potent vehicle for hypergrowth.

BEST PRACTICE: CISCO SYSTEMS

Founded in 1984 by Leonard Bosack and Sandy Lerner, a husband and wife team of academics from Stanford University, as a means of sending data between computers, Cisco has grown to be the company that, according to David Stauffer in *Business the Cisco Way*, is the "company that makes the Internet."

From their first "router" to distribute data, assembled at home, Cisco now develop and manufacture the routers, servers, switches, and software that support the Internet.

Cisco's networking products are designed to connect people, computing devices and computer networks, allowing access or information transfer regardless of differences in time, place or type of computer system.

Cisco provides end-to-end networking solutions that customers use to build their own unified information infrastructure or to connect to an outside network. An end-to-end networking solution is defined as one that provides a common architecture that delivers consistent network services to all users. The broader the range of network services, the more capabilities a network can provide to users connected to it and thus the more effective it is.

Cisco serves customers in three major market areas:

» Large organizations with complex networking needs, spanning multiple locations and with many types of computer systems. Such customers include major corporations, government agencies, pan-governmental organizations, public utilities and educational institutions.
» Service organizations that provide information services, including telecommunication carriers, Internet Service Providers (ISPs), cable companies, and wireless communication providers.
» Other commercial organizations with a need for data networks of their own, as well as connection to the Internet and their business partners and customers.

Cisco operates in over 115 countries using a direct sales force, distributors, value-added resellers and system integrators. The company is headquartered in San Jose, CA. With major operations in Research Triangle Park, NC, and Chelmsford, MA; as well more than 225 sales and support offices in 75 countries.

As a company that is in tune with the individual needs of its customers Cisco does not take a rigid, product-led approach that favors one particular solution regardless of the fit with customer requirements. Cisco's philosophy is to listen to customer needs and then develop solutions for discussion to ensure that those needs are met – a customer-driven approach.

Cisco describes the method of operating as a "global networked business model." A global networked business is an organization, of any size, that uses information and communications strategically to build a network of strong, interactive relationships with all its key constituencies. Such a model is a natural complement to the Internet.

The global networked business model leverages the network for competitive advantage by opening up the corporate information infrastructure to all key constituencies. The global networked business model employs a self-help model of information access that is more efficient and responsive than the traditional model of a few information gatekeepers dispensing data as they see fit. Cisco itself is a leading example of a global networked business. By using networked applications over the Internet and its own internal network, Cisco is seeing financial benefits of nearly $1.4bn a year, while improving customer/partner satisfaction and gaining a competitive advantage. Cisco is now the world's largest Internet commerce site, with 90 percent of its orders transacted over the Web.

Cisco is one of America's greatest corporate hypergrowth success stories. Since its founding in 1986, the company has grown into a global market leader that holds the No. 1 or No. 2 market share in virtually every market segment in which it participates, an achievement shared with Carnival Corporation and Airbus Industrie, two of the case studies in Chapter 7 of this material. Since the IPO in 1990, annual revenues have increased from $69mn to $18.9bn in 2000.

By 2001 Cisco employed approximately 43,000 staff worldwide, about 16,000 of these being in the Bay Area of California.

As covered above, Cisco's IPO (Initial Public Offering) was in 1990. The opening share price was 31 cents but had risen to

$107.12 by the end of 1999 – hypergrowth in value of a staggering 82,300 percent!

Although Cisco deals in cutting-edge technology products, in many ways it is a traditional organization as those products are tangible things, and not the more intangible services that many Internet-related companies have been set up to supply.

There is considerable business sense in being the supplier of the hardware to an expanding tool such as the Internet. In previous periods of rapid growth (see Chapter 3) it has often been the suppliers of components that have been the most successful, provided they could keep up with the technological changes.

Stauffer claims that Cisco in 2000 was the fastest growing firm in the history of the world, having taken only 12 years to reach a market capitalization of $100bn. Achieving this at a time when many Internet companies (especially the dot-com operations) were struggling is no mean achievement.

While huge growth has been predicted for the Internet economy (in 1999 it accounted for $507bn and 2.3 million jobs) it may still be some time before the average person feels comfortable with making a majority of their purchases online. Security of payment is often quoted as being a major barrier. The companies that are trading successfully online – Amazon.com is one of the best known – do not find that getting into profit is easy. However, as a supplier of the resources necessary for Internet operations, Cisco do not face that problem.

If Internet trading has been slower than predicted, Internet use is growing at a fantastic rate. With over 2000 new Websites being registered each month there is ample evidence that few, if any, traditional companies are ignoring the Internet. While a Web address on business cards, letter heading, or on the side of a delivery truck would have been rare even as late as 1996, now there might be comment if it were not present.

Every organization that experiences hypergrowth tends to have the name of an individual attached to it. Bill Gates at Microsoft, Richard Branson at Virgin, Ted Arison at Carnival. Cisco is no different. Linked to its spectacular growth is the name of John

Chambers, the CEO. Chambers is responsible for the fact that Cisco sales in business-to-business e-commerce are over $32mn per day.

Aged 51 in 2001, Chambers is not one of the young "whiz kids" of the Internet but an experienced manager, trained in law and marketing.

Chambers' philosophy can be read in detail in Stauffer's book, but five areas stand out when considering the hypergrowth of the company.

Vision

It is rare to find a growing company that is not populated by people with vision and a sense of mission. Chambers certainly finds this important. Part of the importance is the internal motivation that mission and vision provide, but they also transmit a good feeling to customers and potential customers. They may well, as an added bonus, scare competitors. The CEO needs to be the one who holds the vision tight and disseminates it through the organization. Once the buzz starts it can be quickly transmitted both to employees and those outwith (a much-used Scottish word that is very appropriate here) the organization.

Customers

No organization can exist without customers and hypergrowth is impossible without the cooperation of the customer base. Cisco works hard at maintaining its customer loyalty – a loyalty that no organization, however large, can ever take for granted. Putting the needs of the customer first is a key to growth. The only sustainable growth is through the customer. Neglect the customer and growth ceases. Chambers is one of those who believes passionately in listening to the customer.

Acquisitions

Some companies acquire others in a haphazard manner. It some-times does not seem to matter whether the acquisition fits into the core business or not. Cisco (and Chambers) acquired those companies that had similar visions to that of Cisco. Integrating a new company can be very difficult if it has a different philosophy and culture. If they are similar, however, the task of integration and thus an earlier contribution to profits is much easier.

Cisco has grown by acquisition. Three companies were acquired in 1994, four the next year, seven in 1996, six in 1997, nine in 1998, no less than 18 in 1999 and six more in 2000. Added to the original Cisco, this made for a group made up of 54 components by the millennium.

Using the Internet internally

Cisco is a company that has made maximum internal use of the Internet. The rapidity of communications made possible by the Internet allows Cisco managers to make and communicate decisions with a speed that would astonish many more traditional organizations. Cisco use the Internet not only for taking orders but for hiring staff – this alone means that the cost of hiring is 40 percent lower than the industry average – and then training them. Given Cisco's intimate involvement with the Internet, using the net internally sends out a powerful message to customers.

Putting people first

Tom Peters and Bob Waterman coined the term "productivity through people" in their 1982 book, *In Search of Excellence*. No matter how advanced the technology, ultimately success and growth depend on people. Cisco has adopted this maxim from its earliest days. The company looks for people who will be more than satisfactory; they demand and get the best. Anybody who does not make the mark does not stay. There is no room in hypergrowth operations for non-performers.

Having acquired the best Cisco makes them part of the team, provides the necessary training and recognizes excellence. In this way people pass on the vision.

By listening to customers, ensuring that the company delivers and that it is staffed by the right people Cisco has shown a degree of hypergrowth that has astonished industry analysts. As the Internet grows even more rapidly, companies like Cisco that remain at the cutting edge are likely to continue to grow with it.

KEY LEARNING POINTS

» Despite the wonders of technology, people are still the most important resource available to an organization.

» The developments of the Internet and e-commerce do not relieve organizations from the traditional management tasks but those tasks can be accomplished in different ways and more quickly.

» Technological advances can be exploited by those companies that are at the cutting edge.

» High technology developments leave no place for the "me too" organization.

The Global Dimension of Hypergrowth

This chapter discusses how:

» Hypergrowth will often involve organizations moving into global markets.
» The globalization aspects of hypergrowth are political and social issues, in addition to economic ones.
» Inducements are often offered by governments in order to attract expanding foreign companies.
» As Nike discovered, consumers in the developed world are increasingly concerned about human rights.
» Growing globally involves taking on board new methods of doing business that are in tune with local culture reasons for going global.

Hypergrowth, as defined in Chapter 2, often results in organizations expanding beyond their original national borders and catering to new customer bases. It may be possible for organizations in very large countries such as the US or China to experience hypergrowth purely within a national context, but they are the exception. In recent times the issue of globalization has meant that companies have assisted hypergrowth by moving production to lower cost areas, often by contracting it out. This has become more than just an economic issue as it has both social and political implications.

Not all governments and economies are as large and powerful as those of the US, the major European powers or Japan. Ellwood (2001) in his work on globalization provides figures to show that of the 100 largest economies of the world, multinational corporations account for 50 percent. In fact, he quotes figures that show that the "economy" of General Motors is larger than that of Norway, a relatively rich European nation, and considerably larger than that of Greece. Not only General Motors but also Ford, Mitsui, Mitsubishi, Itichu, Shell, and Mauruberi have individual annual sales revenues greater than the GDP (gross domestic product) of Greece. Perhaps even more surprising is that the sales revenue of Wal-Mart exceeded the GDP of Israel by about $10bn in 1997, a figure that has doubtless increased since Wal-Mart acquired the UK supermarket giant Asda in 2000.

To the opponents of globalization, however, the issues are far deeper than pure revenue. Their concerns center around the removal of fiscal and political independence from governments and the apparent transfer of power to the larger corporations in the world, a point argued eloquently by David Korten in *When Corporations Rule the World* (1996). To such opponents, globalization is more than just similar products being available on a global basis; to them it is actually the integration of the global economy by the dismantling of trade and political barriers and the increasing political and economic power of multinational corporations.

GOVERNMENTS AND HYPERGROWTH

Just like individuals and companies, countries have to earn money before they can spend it. In order to acquire goods and services from outside their own borders it is necessary to earn foreign currency.

The US, UK, Germany etc. – i.e. the developed nations – are able to earn foreign currency using a mixture of exporting raw materials and manufactured goods and by providing services to other countries. Many developing countries are more dependent on raw materials and are particularly vulnerable to a fall in prices if they are dependent upon a single resource or crop. Earning foreign currency by providing services requires the development of expertise which can take a great deal of time and therefore the development of a manufacturing capability is seen as a useful addition to the economy as it lessens the dependence upon a small number of raw materials or crops. Countries that rely on a single raw material or crop for earning foreign exchange can be affected disastrously by a slump in world demand or a bad harvest, as they have no means of diversifying and earning income by alternative means.

Governments tend to welcome manufacturing companies because they not only provide goods for export in many instances but because they provide employment. No government can afford to ignore the social condition of its citizens for long – to do so is likely to lead to the fall of the government through elections in democratic regimes and revolution in totalitarian ones. A government must be seen to be assisting people with jobs especially if the economy is stagnant and there is high unemployment. High employment rates mean that the government has to do less in terms of welfare policy, but once the unemployment rate begins to rise the population require action and support – support that must be paid for out of taxation or foreign loans.

In order to assist increasing employment it is not unusual for governments to offer considerable inducements for companies to set up operations in an area of high unemployment. The inducements can range from tax breaks, through training and building grants, to the provision of infrastructure construction. That governments are keen to assist business in providing economic growth is evidenced by the fact that according to Klein (2000), the proportion of corporate taxation as a percentage of total federal revenue in the US dropped from 32 percent in 1952 to 11.5 percent in 1998. Even a government as apparently wealthy as that of the US uses tax inducements to secure employment. Encouraging companies by decreasing taxation presents governments with a dilemma. If corporate taxes fall then how is the shortfall to be made up? Squaring the circle helps – as more people are in work both the need to spend on welfare decreases and the yield from income taxes should increase. This makes economic sense and provided that wages are sufficient so that they do not need any form of government top up, thus eating into the tax yield, the system may well work. If, however, the inducements are so large that individual taxes have to be increased, then a vicious circle can begin. It is no use reducing property and business taxes for a company to relocate if the personal and property taxes of those gaining employment have to be raised to a level that nobody who works at the new factory can afford to live in the area.

The perceived wisdom is that encouraging organizations into an area will rejuvenate the economy and lead to a rise in prosperity for not just the workers at the enterprise but shopkeepers, bus drivers, plumbers, carpenters etc. – all will eventually benefit. Provided that the wages paid are sufficient and that the jobs are permanent, the above is indeed the case. Where job insecurity still exists and only low wages are paid, however, then general prosperity is less likely to rise and may actually decrease.

In countries like the UK with minimum wage regulations that can and are enforced by the courts this is less likely to happen, but then some companies will not relocate to such a jurisdiction. Relocation itself suggests that unless there is a huge increase in demand leading to extra production it is likely that one area's gain has been another's loss.

Ellwood quotes an *LA Times* report stating that prior to the formation of NAFTA in 1995, the Jean's manufacturer Guess? Inc. was producing 97 percent of its product in Los Angeles. By 1997 this figure was down to 35 percent with 1000 jobs being lost in LA. The company had relocated mainly to Mexico where it opened five factories. Mexico, also a NAFTA member, has a lower average wage rate and as there will be no import restrictions in moving the product into the US, it made economic sense to relocate production to a lower cost area. Corporations are not primarily in the social care business, they are expected to make a profit for their owners – the investors – and that means increasing profits and/or cutting costs.

EPZs

A considerable amount of the foreign direct investment (FDI) into developing nations has been into operations in export (or economic) processing zones (EPZs) – areas set up by governments where raw materials are imported and finished products manufactured and exported free of any customs duties. Developed from the freeport concept, EPZs are almost mini-economies of their own. They are located in the boundaries of the country but are not subject to all of its laws. The goods produced vary from clothes to consumer electronics and the advantage for the manufacturer or assembler is that they are able to operate free from many of the custom's restrictions they might face in a more traditional environment. Klein (2000) has profiled the operation of such zones in the Philippines and concludes that the ones she studied operated at very low wage rates combined with harsh working conditions.

One of the major issues facing governments promoting EPZs is that of the "swallows." These are companies that move in and take advantage of tax exemptions, grants etc. and then move to another similar area if better inducements are offered. This does nothing for the long-term prosperity of an area or for job security. In fact its effect is very negative because in order to attract another company, even more inducements have to be made and workers may be required to accept even lower wages and longer hours. Being a "swallow" may result in an increase in profits and short-term growth for the company but not only will there be financial costs associated with relocation but also the loss of trained workers, which may result in a dip in quality and consequently a loss of customers.

CULTURE

Culture, defined as "the way things are done around here," is the outward manifestation of the values, attitudes and beliefs of particular social groups and populations. As an organization expands further and further away from its original home area, cultural sensitivity becomes more and more important.

Products and operating practices may well need to be altered to meet the cultural needs of a new market. These issues are covered in detail in *Managing Diversity* and *Going Global*, companion texts in this series.

The difference in cultural norms and methods of conducting business may be considerable and a number of books and articles covering these areas have been produced, examples of which are included in Chapter 9.

Any organization expanding outwith its own cultural area should ensure that all staff are aware of any cultural sensitivities and are able to adapt their behavior to the new area rather than expecting others to adapt to them.

BEST PRACTICE: NIKE

It is not unusual to be asked during Trivial Pursuit games "who was the Greek goddess of victory?" While the answer may not be on the tip of everybody's tongue it may well be on their foot or their chest, because it is Nike – also one of the best known brand names in the sports clothing/leisure fashion market.

Since Phil Knight first thought about breaking the German domination of the US athletic shoe industry in 1962, Nike has become a global brand. Its logo (which cost the company a mere $35), "the swoosh" has gained worldwide recognition on a par with the Shell patina and the Coca-Cola bottle.

Nike's hypergrowth has not been without controversy, especially in regard to its contract factories in the developing world. This issue is covered later in this section together with the efforts Nike has made to answer its critics and be transparent about its business practices.

As mentioned earlier, Phil Knight had produced a research paper on breaking the German domination of the US athletic shoe market. Knight, an athlete himself, had attended Stanford Business School in the 1960s after meeting the coach of the University of Oregon athletics team, Bill Bowerman, in 1957.

In 1962 Knight decided to import shoes from the Japanese Onishuka Tiger Company and set up his Blue Ribbon Sports (BRS) operation. Involving Bowerman, they each contributed $500 and sold 1300 pairs of shoes gaining $8000 in revenue. Taking on their first employee (Jeff Johnson, also an athlete), they opened the first retail outlet in 1966 and the following year designed the Marathon shoe to be made in Japan. By 1969 the company had 20 employees and took in $300,000 in revenue.

The famous Swoosh logo was designed by a student, Carolyn Davidson in 1971 – she received a fee of $35!

The Nike brand

The decision to adopt the catchy Nike brand name was made in 1972. A Greek name, easy to pronounce and signifying a connection with victory was a masterstroke for a company involved with the sporting fraternity. Even the logo gives an impression of speed and also looks like a tick – thus signifying correctness.

Throughout the 1970s a succession of US sports stars began to use Nike shoes – Steve Prefontaine (who unfortunately died prematurely in 1975) and John McEnroe being two of the best known. By 1974 revenues were nearly $5mn.

Nike's IPO (Initial Public Offering) was in 1980, the year in which revenue topped $269mn and the company had 2700 employees. The revenue figure rose to nearly $920mn in 1984, the year in which Carl Lewis won four Olympic Gold Medals wearing Nike shoes. Of considerable importance was the $158mn contribution of foreign sales revenue. Nike was beginning to cater for a global market.

The 1980s were difficult times for Nike. Revenues topped $1bn in 1986, having dipped the previous year triggering a cost reduction program, but they dipped again in 1987. The purchasing of sports shoes was beginning to move out of the athletics market, however, and onto the fashion scene. The days of the designer label had arrived in the mass market and Nike was well placed to benefit.

Nike opened their first Nike Town outlet in 1990, the year revenue passed the $2bn mark, reaching $3bn the year after with international revenues reaching $1bn in 1992.

With more and more major stars using Nike shoes, not least of all Michael Jordan, revenues increased to just under $5bn in 1995. The global nature of Nike was shown by a series of Europe-specific advertisements using French soccer star Eric Cantona (later of Manchester United, the highly successful UK soccer club) in 1995 following the opening of a European distribution center the previous year.

Whatever they are called, sport shoes, sneakers, trainers (in the UK), Nike and the Swoosh are now a global brand. Nike Equipment Division was formed in 1996 to produce hockey skates, eyewear, sport watches, protective clothing, balls etc. With a full apparel range Nike was able to raise revenues to $6.5bn, nearly a third of which was derived from non-shoe products.

Opening Customer Service Centers in Asia in 1997 Nike made major inroads into the Asian market, especially in China, so that revenues for the early years of the millennium are tipped to exceed $10bn.

An increase from $8000 to $10bn in less than 40 years is hypergrowth indeed, considering the nature of the product. What might be expected in computers is unexpected in footwear.

Nike have grown by carefully matching the product to the customer and using major names and icons to promote those products. Expansion has been rational, moving into new markets and products that can benefit from existing ones and keeping costs as low as possible.

Nike and globalization
The issue of globalization was referred to earlier in this chapter.

In May 1997, the CEO of Nike, Phil Knight, was picketed during a speech at his alma mater – Stanford Business School. The protestors were students concerned at conditions in the contract factories supplying Nike.

As was covered earlier, many of the most famous brand names are actually produced by contractors, often in the developing world. Companies have a duty to their shareholders to maximize income and therefore seek the lowest cost production facilities commensurate with maintaining quality.

Klein, in *No Logo*, reports on an almost global (at least in the developed world) anti-Nike movement. At issue was the wages and conditions paid to those producing Nike-branded goods – wages and conditions that it appeared to the protestors to be abysmally low.

Nike responded to the protests by meeting with protestors, especially those in poorer areas and at least appearing to be listening to them. In 1998 Knight himself announced closer monitoring of wages and conditions. It is not for the writer of this material to comment on the conditions in contract factories. It is, however, worthy of note that the issues are addressed directly on Nike's Website. That site includes details of factories together with photographs. Knight himself has expressed the view that Nike fundamentally believes that human rights and good business practices can peacefully co-exist.

Nike claim that every contract factory is monitored both externally (provided by PricewaterhouseCoopers) and internally by Nike. An action plan is published in response to each effort. Nike has promised to be transparent in its monitoring efforts, thus are providing action plans to show the progress made in response the original monitoring activities. It is easy enough to find details of the reports on the Website so it would seem that Nike have listened to their customer concerns about working conditions and have acted on them. Nike claim that it continuously strives to fully implement its Code of Conduct throughout the supply chain thus taking the leadership role in making real changes for the workers in the factories operated by its contractors.

Rhetoric is easy but the fact that the company is so transparent suggests a real commitment. This is good as it is not only shareholders who should benefit from hypergrowth but also customers and employees. If the latter benefit then the economy of which they are part also benefits and more customers are generated for the company's products.

Globalization, as shown by the riots at the G8 Summit talks in Genoa in July 2001 is an emotive issue. Companies involved in global operations need to take the concerns raised by globalization seriously.

Nike sponsor a large number of sporting events including many for charity – again examples can be found on the Nike Website (see Chapter 9). Sport is one of the areas that bring people in a divided world together and any efforts to involve more people should be applauded. Nike's hypergrowth has mirrored that of international sport and as that grows, so too will Nike.

KEY LEARNING POINTS

» Hypergrowth will often involve expansion into new geographic areas.

» Expanding into new geographic areas involves taking on board different cultures.

» Governments may well offer inducements to encourage organizations to move into an area.

» Consumers are increasingly concerned about the welfare of those who produce the products they buy.

Hypergrowth Strategies:
The State of the Art

This chapter explores the following current trends:

» Strategy can be a plan, a ploy, a pattern, a position or a perspective.
» Improperly managed hypergrowth can be destructive.
» Hypergrowth leads to increased profits and power.
» Hypergrowth provides the company with considerable bargaining power with both its suppliers and customers – power that should be used fairly.
» The survival of suppliers is important to the hypergrowth company.
» Wage costs can be cut by relocation.
» Joint ventures, franchises, mergers, and acquisitions are means of entering new markets.
» Cashflow can easily become a problem during rapid expansion as exposure increases.
» Customers, their gaining and retention are the ultimate factor in hypergrowth.

WHAT IS STRATEGY?

According to the great Henry Mintzberg of McGill University, "strategy" is not just one thing but can have a number of definitions contingent on the circumstances, or may be a combination of all of them. Perhaps the most common use of the word is to mean a *plan*. The vast majority of dictionaries use this definition and the concept of strategy as a plan is the most appropriate to this discussion of hypergrowth. The other components of Mintzberg's ideas on strategy, however, are also relevant to hypergrowth.

According to Mintzberg, strategy can also be a *ploy*, a *pattern*, a *position*, and a *perspective*. The use of ploys, specific maneuvers that look like part of a strategy but are really designed to outwit an opponent, are well known in military circles. Field Marshal Montgomery, the commander of the UK forces for the invasion of France in 1944 was well known for using ploys. He would convince his enemy that he was going to attack a particular area, wait until the enemy had brought up reinforcements and then attack where the reinforcements had come from, thus exploiting a weakness.

Ploys also have a role in business strategy. They can be used to fool competitors into developing in a particular way to block somebody, only to find that they have been misled and have missed a window of opportunity. Automobile manufacturers are well known for "leaking" details of new products that are not always correct but which wrong-foot the competition.

As strategy exists within a timeframe it also develops a pattern or a consistency over a period. This allows for predictions on future behavior to be made as a result of studying the way a strategy has evolved. One can say that strategy is not a fixed point but a moving pattern – a pattern that will also contain currents and undertows, some of which may be ploys.

As a position, strategy is concerned with where the organization positions itself within the external environment/market. The relationship with the external environment is key to the derivation of an acceptable and successful strategy and is particularly important in the case of hypergrowth as hypergrowth has implications for the wider environment that surrounds the organization.

Finally, strategy as a perspective relates to the way the organization perceives the environment in which it operates. Strategy needs to be contingent upon the environment. It is only the very largest of organizations that can operate irrespective of their environment – most organizations will find that the environment imposes constraints on what they can and cannot do.

THE MANAGEMENT OF HYPERGROWTH

The general principles associated with the management of the growth process are covered in detail in *Managing Growth*, a complementary title in the *ExpressExec* series, and so this chapter concentrates on the specific strategies required to promote and then manage the hypergrowth process.

Rapid growth can cause major disruption to the smooth operation of an organization and if not managed efficiently can be highly destructive. The difference between a nuclear reactor and a nuclear bomb lies in the degree of external control of the process. The former is controlled and provides a useable source of energy over a period. The latter follows the same scientific principles but in an uncontrolled manner and is highly destructive. The runaway reaction of the nuclear bomb cannot be reversed once it is set off. Organizations need to control and manage hypergrowth in the same way.

STRATEGIC FACTORS PROMOTING HYPERGROWTH

The organizations that feature as cases in this material – Cisco, Nike, Carnival Corporation, Airbus Industrie, and Samsung – have pursued strategies that have been highly successful but were certainly not accidental – they resulted from an in-depth knowledge of the markets for the organization's products and services. It is that in-depth knowledge and an understanding of exactly what it is that the customer wants that are prerequisites for hypergrowth. Possessing them does not ensure hypergrowth but it can be guaranteed that a company that ignores them will never achieve anything like hypergrowth.

With the exception of *Airbus Industrie,* it would have been possible to use one or two of each company's competitors as cases, because they are in a hypergrowth sector. Reebok or Adidas could have replaced

Nike; there are a number of Internet-related companies that have been highly successful although perhaps none have been quoted as actually defining the way the Internet operates like Cisco has; Royal Caribbean International or Star Cruises of Asia, both companies that have experienced extraordinary growth though not to the extent of becoming the world market leader as Carnival has; Toshiba or Sony could have replaced Samsung, such has been the growth in consumer electronics – growth that seems set to continue for many years to come.

Airbus Industrie is slightly different in that it was predicted (as stated in the case study in Chapter 7) that they (Airbus is a consortium) could not make any inroads into what was fast becoming a Boeing hegemony of the civil airliner market. That Airbus now vies with Boeing for the number 1 spot is testimony to the way the organization has built up its market share.

Hypergrowth occurs when a company's or companies' market share rises far quicker than that of competitors. It may well be, as in the case of the consumer electronics or cruise markets that the whole market is growing so quickly as to provide opportunities for more than one company to experience hypergrowth. In a slower growing market there is still the possibility that a company can put all the factors required for hypergrowth into place so effectively that it can grow rapidly to dominate that market – as Wal-Mart has done in the US supermarket sector.

Hypergrowth has become such a dominant feature in recent years because improvements in communication and the breaking down of trade barriers have allowed companies to respond extremely rapidly to new technologies or emerging markets. People get to know about things far quicker than ever before. Fashions and logos become recognizable at the speed of light, i.e. the speed of a television signal. When an athlete wearing Nike shoes wins an international race the image is beamed around the world at light speed (literally). In previous times it might have taken months or even years for a logo or a brand to travel from Australia to the US or the UK. The Sydney Olympics, shown as they were in real time, meant that images were being seen as they happened. This is one of the major reasons why hypergrowth is more common today than it has been.

WHY SHOULD AN ORGANIZATION WANT HYPERGROWTH?

Hypergrowth is not just a feature of private companies with a profit motive. The public sector can also undergo hypergrowth, often providing growth opportunities for private companies. The increase in publicly provided housing in the UK in the 1950s onwards not only brought into being much larger local government departments but also provided huge growth opportunities for companies in the building industry. Local government had to learn how to deal with huge spending departments, some of which having revenues that were large enough for them to lend overnight on the international money markets. Local government had not been used to needing employees with such skills and there was a requirement for huge recruitment drives to acquire the caliber of people needed.

In the main, however, the days of big government appear to be over. Current trends are for the state to be less of an actual provider of services and more a facilitator and purchaser of them from the private sector. From the point of its election in 1997, the UK Labour Party government under Tony Blair made much of its intention to use public-private partnerships to build (and even operate) schools, hospitals, transport systems etc.

For the rest of this chapter, however, the hypergrowth will be assumed to be within the private sector and in companies and corporations where the main objective is profit and a return on stockholder investment. The same hypergrowth strategies are just as applicable to the public sector.

Companies and corporations welcome hypergrowth because of the perception that they will make more profit and thus be more attractive to investors.

This is a reasonable perception provided that the hypergrowth is managed efficiently. If, however, it is poorly managed the company may well end up in trouble despite rapid growth, as will be shown later in the sections on finance and resources.

It is also true that the larger an organization is the more power it can wield and the more it can dictate to its suppliers in order to obtain the discounts that economies of scale can offer. If a company buys 9 percent of one supplier's product, the company is highly dependent on that supplier to deliver on time. If it buys 90 percent, it can dictate the terms because if it withdraws its business then the supplier will have a major problem. Many suppliers often express delight at gaining a huge contract with a large corporation only to be dismayed later on as that corporation begins to drive down the price. No organization should ever be completely dependent on another.

Just occasionally there are companies that do not want to grow – their owners are happy with them as they are. The danger in not growing, however, is being a target for acquisition by those who are. Hypergrowth is normally presented as a positive thing. For the individual who has not considered its implications it can be threatening. In a hypergrowth situation, change can occur rapidly and change is often uncomfortable. Senior managers should be aware that hypergrowth may produce fear in employees as well as pleasure and pride.

THE MARKETPLACE

A market is a place where exchange takes place. In medieval times, farmers, weavers, silversmiths etc. would bring their goods to a central point, normally the market square in a town, and meet with potential buyers and an exchange of goods for money (or other goods in a barter system) would take place. Today's markets are considerably more complex and yet the same basic transaction occurs: the corporation has a product or service to sell and the potential customers have to spend. There may be a number of suppliers, most with very similar basic products trying to attract new customers and to retain their existing ones. The scenario is no different in concept to a row of barrows in a farmers' market. The customers examine the goods on offer and then make their choice depending on their requirements, budgets, personal preferences, and previous experiences.

The six components of the market are the:

» supplier
» supplier's suppliers
» customer (or potential customer)
» helpers
» competitors
» external environment.

The helpers include advertising agencies, banks, investors, trucking firms – all those who assist the supplier with the means to deliver what the customer wants to where the customer wants it.

In respect of those who supply raw materials, consumables, components etc. to the supplier for processing into a product or service; the supplier is their customer.

The external environment encompasses governments (local, regional, national and even pan-national institutions such as the EU or NAFTA), in fact anybody or anything whose actions can impinge upon the supplier's activities. Each organization has a different external environment depending on the nature of their activities. For example, a hurricane in the Caribbean is part of the external environment and yet is unlikely to affect Nike's business to a great extent. It is an important factor for Carnival (Chapter 7) as many of their cruises feature the Caribbean.

The supplier's suppliers and the value chain

Very few companies achieve hypergrowth without the help of others. Most transactions comprise a value chain where value is added at each step until the end user pays for the product or service (see Fig. 6.1).

MAXIMIZING BARGAINING POWER

Size permits a company to reduce costs by employing its bargaining power (a concept described by Michael Porter as one of his forces of competition).

What is important is the balance between the relative bargaining power of suppliers, and customers. Suppliers will want to deliver the minimum quality acceptable to the customer for the highest price that the customer will pay. This is common sense – there is no point in higher quality or specification than the customer actually wants (note the use of the words "minimum acceptable") because this only costs money that cannot be recouped as the customer will not wish to pay for something they did not want – they will accept it gratefully if it is free (or at least appears to be free).

The customer of course would like the highest possible quality and specification for the lowest price that the supplier will accept.

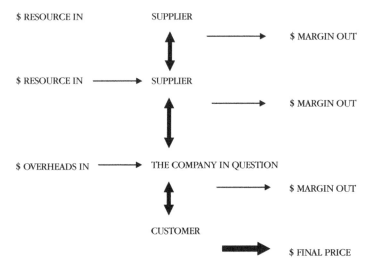

Fig. 6.1

Somewhere between these two extremes there will be a meeting of minds. The customer will pay what the supplier can afford to charge while still making a profit, provided that it is within the customer's budget.

In a business situation each supplier is also a customer of its suppliers and if it is buying in large quantities, as happens during hypergrowth, it can demand lower prices. Equally if demand is high it can actually charge more to its customers. In the late 1990s the demand for "Toy Story" merchandise was so great in the UK that there were pre-Christmas news items of parents flying to the US to buy at premium prices! If somebody wants something badly enough they may be prepared to pay a premium.

Once a company goes into hypergrowth its bargaining power over its suppliers increases dramatically. It may even have power over governments, as will be shown in the next section.

How a company decides to use its power will say a great deal about the values it holds. The temptation is to gain the lowest possible price. It is worth remembering, however, that the company needs its suppliers as much as its suppliers need its business. Screw down the price too much and it may be impossible for the supplier to make a reasonable profit. The supplier's only option may be to cut corners and then the quality delivered begins to suffer – as does the receiving company. Suppliers who are treated properly will be more likely to cooperate with the company in raising quality.

An important business issue in recent years has been the time taken by large companies to pay their suppliers for goods and services. The longer the company can take, the more interest it can accrue on the money and the easier cashflow is to manage. Small business do not have the cash reserves of larger ones and can be driven to the edge of bankruptcy or beyond if their customers are dilatory about paying on time. The situation has become so bad in the UK that the government is considering taking action. Many companies offer discounts for prompt payment but it appears that large customers demand such discounts whether they pay on time or not.

MOVING TO A LOW COST AREA

The more costs can be cut, the more likely it will be that hypergrowth can be achieved. Profit is the difference between costs and revenue (in simplistic terms). Revenue is raised by increasing prices or (better still) increasing the customer base. Costs can be cut by moving to a lower wage economy either in the company's own name or through outside contracting. Wages can represent over 80 percent of a company's cost and so have a considerable influence on profit.

As covered in the previous chapter of this material, governments welcome investment especially in depressed areas as this should help reduce dependency on their welfare programs. There are thus considerable inducements offered to companies to relocate to such areas.

Many of the major manufacturing names in the developed world now have their products made for them by contractors in the developing world (with all the issues raised in Chapter 5). This means that the contractor carries more of the risks for the ventures and thus fuels the company's growth as they have less need to spend on manufacturing facilities.

Governments may enter into partnership with companies in depressed areas to rejuvenate the economy. This is not a new concept. In the 1930s both Theodore Roosevelt in the US and Adolph Hitler in Nazi Germany began huge public works programs to put people back to work in order to beat the effects of the great depression.

COMPETITION BETWEEN EXISTING SUPPLIERS

As would be expected, the greatest competition comes between the current players in a particular market. Even where prices are very much the same there is competition on levels of service, supplementary products and geographic provision. It may be difficult for a single company or perhaps just a few to achieve hypergrowth in such a scenario unless the market is also undergoing hypergrowth. The success of the Carnival Group in the cruise industry is in part due to the fact that the whole market was growing rapidly so that the major players could also grow at a very fast pace.

Acquisitions, mergers and joint ventures

While competition between existing suppliers can appear cut-throat, they will often come together to cooperate on safety issues and to defend the market from new entrants. As more and more projects become global then they may be beyond the capacity of a single supplier and alliances and joint ventures will be set up. This can be an excellent method of expanding into either a new market or new technology in a way that spreads the risk.

Many of the large projects that have been so prevalent in the years since the Second World War, such as Concorde, the Channel Tunnel and the International Space Station, are beyond the resources of any one organization. Companies such as Boeing which closely guarded its proprietary information have been forced to share expertise. As Sabbach (1995) has shown, the Boeing 777 has required Boeing to work with a host of subcontractors across the world in order to produce a competitive product. These subcontractors bear part of the financial risk and the spreading of such risk is a trade off to the loss of the proprietary information.

The balance between competition and cooperation is a delicate one and not all such alliances survive in the long term. A full consideration of strategic alliances can be found in *Strategic Alliances* by Peter Lorange and Johan Roos (see Chapter 9).

The strategy of hypergrowth through acquisition and merger is one that is often employed. Carnival (see Chapter 7) has grown rapidly by acquiring its competitors, often retaining their brand names and their loyal customer base. Acquisition (or merger) can remove competition if the organizations are competing for the same market, or it can allow for a smoother movement into a new market or area of operation. A glance at the history of many of today's huge corporations will show how they have grown by acquiring rivals or others in businesses where there is a synergy present.

There seem to be times when there is a frenzy of acquisitions and mergers. One company may be bidding for another while at the same time defending itself from a bid from another company. Most governments have agencies in place to ensure a degree of fairness in this process. What the bidder is actually acquiring is an ownership interest through stock and the unscrupulous have been known to try and manipulate the stock markets to their own advantage.

Both acquisitions and mergers involve the absorption of new people, ideas, suppliers and customers. Many are successful but there are times when a divorce occurs as quickly as the marriage. Successful hypergrowth requires the company to look very carefully at any possible acquisitions and to ensure that they fit into the overall plans for the organization and will complement them and aid profits.

Licensing/franchises

British Airways has been a major player in the franchising of airline products as a means of growing its market share. By franchising off BA, the franchisee airline is able to benefit from the economies of scale in training, supplies etc. of a much bigger player. Organizations can license or franchise from an existing player in order to gain a foothold into a new market although if they are not already conversant with that market, any franchisor may be reluctant to allow their name to be used. The growth of McDonald's on a global basis has been through franchise agreements. It is a very low risk method (for the franchisor) of achieving fast, even hyper-, growth for a relatively small outlay often offset by the payments from franchises.

RESOURCES AND FINANCE

Weitzen (1991) stresses the point that one of the worst things that can happen to a company is to run out of cash. Any form of growth usually means investing ahead of revenue. In a hypergrowth situation the investment might be very large and the company can be very exposed to cashflow problems before the revenue comes on stream. This is one reason why the beginnings of hypergrowth can be a dangerous time as a cash rich predator may be able to attract the company into a merger or even giving up its independence using its cash reserves as a lure.

Hypergrowth can generate massive profits but prudence in looking after the money should never be forgotten. The more profit that will be made, the more resources may have to bought up front.

CUSTOMERS

Ultimately hypergrowth depends on customers. Hypergrowth companies know their customer base. They give customers what the customer wants and not just what the company thinks they want. Money spent on researching the market is never wasted.

Hypergrowth is often to be found at the cutting edge of new technologies but always a little behind. Hypergrowth companies do not dash in until the majority of bugs are eliminated. They test and retest to ensure that the quality is high. Hypergrowth companies have good customer care policies – they do not quibble about refunds. They make ''friends'' with the customer because they know that word of mouth recommendations are far more effective than advertising and cost nothing.

Hypergrowth cannot occur without the help of the customer base. A massive increase in profits requires an expansion of the customer base. Whether the expansion is at home or abroad (where the company will need to operate to different cultural norms) does not matter in the long term. What does matter is firstly gaining new customers and, equally important, the retention of both old and new customers so that they continue to spend their money with the company and not with its competitors.

HYPERGROWTH NOW

The August 2001 PricewaterhouseCoopers report mentioned in Chapter 3 (see also Chapter 9) found a variety of challenges and concerns among the Fortune 1000 companies that are currently launching and operating e-business initiatives in an attempt to achieve or continue hypergrowth:

Over half of the CEOs of the fastest growing companies in the US stated that their business and industry sector was being driven by cost control and strategies for coping with the business slowdown and recession. However defensive the outlook of the majority, a substantial minority see their business and sector as being driven by offense-related factors like e-business and globalization with growth likely to be, they believe, considerably above the predicted norm.

The top factors driving their business and industry sector in 2001 according to the CEOs of fast growth companies were believed to be:

» cost reduction and containment – 55%
» strategies to deal with the business slowdown – 50%.

Other drivers were reported to be:

» worker shortages – 39%
» actions of the Federal Reserve Board – 28%
» e-commerce and the Internet – 22%
» intellectual asset management – 21%
» mergers and acquisitions – 18%
» globalization – 14%
» tax cuts for individuals – 12%.

(PricewaterhouseCoopers Trendsetter survey, August 2001)

It is interesting to note that there were considerable differences between the priorities of CEOs in differing sectors. E-commerce was a greater priority for those in the service sector as were the actions of the Federal Reserve. Different growth sectors will have different priorities.

KEY LEARNING POINTS

» While hypergrowth is about increasing profits, it can only happen by gaining and retaining customers.

» The value chain cannot be ignored as hypergrowth also depends upon the relationships the company has with its suppliers.

» Wage costs are the largest proportion of most company's costs and can be cut by relocation.

» Inducements are nearly always available to encourage relocation.

» Competitors may become partners in joint ventures. Markets are dynamic not static – last year's competitor may be this year's partner.

Hypergrowth Success Stories

What are the secrets of hypergrowth? This chapter explains the phenomenon of hypergrowth by case studies on:

» Carnival Group;
» Airbus Industrie; and
» Samsung.

The success case studies in this chapter feature the Carnival Corporation of the US, which has grown to be the number one cruise operator in the world from just one ship in the late 1960s; Airbus Industrie, like Carnival founded in the 1960s and currently the world's joint number one maker of commercial aircraft; and Samsung, a Korean electronics giant, once again founded in the 1960s and now a global presence in both electronics and telecommunications.

CASE 1: CARNIVAL CORPORATION

The Carnival Corporation of the US is a hypergrowth organization in a hypergrowth industry. The global cruise market, of which Carnival is by far and way the market leader, increased from 5 million annual customers to nearly 10 million between 1993 and 2000; 75 percent of those customers are from the US.

When Carnival Cruises' first vessel, the *Mardi Gras* (the ex-Canadian Pacific liner, *Empress of Canada*), left Miami on her maiden cruise in 1972 she went aground. One competing company even offered its customers a drink named "Mardi Gras on the Rocks." Hardly an auspicious start for a new venture. However by 2001, Carnival was not only successful it was the market leader in the fastest growing sector of the tourism industry.

Ted Arison had been a colonel in the Israeli army and had then been involved in the air charter business. In 1966 he joined forces with a Norwegian, Knut Kloster who had a new passenger ship, the *Sunward*, laid up in Europe. The cruise industry was just beginning to boom in the US and Arison suggested basing the *Sunward* at the then small port of Miami. Together Kloster and Arison formed Norwegian Caribbean Line (NCL), a company that became Norwegian Cruise Lines eventually being owned by Star Cruises of Thailand.

NCL was very successful but in 1971 Arison and Kloster split up. Kloster remained with NCL and Arison acquired the *Empress of Canada*, a surplus to requirements Atlantic liner, and renamed her *Mardi Gras*. As mentioned earlier, the *Mardi Gras*' first voyage in 1972 was marred by going aground but other maiden voyages and cruises have suffered mishaps (none as great as the *Titanic*'s in 1912), P&O's new superliner *Aurora* breaking down on her maiden cruise in 2000 being an example.

Arison enabled the growth of Carnival by two means. The first was by offering a product to a new segment of the market – the younger vacationer – and secondly by acquiring well-known brands.

Carnival's growth

(Note: the size of passenger ships is given by their GRT (gross registered tonnage). This is a measure of volume not weight and comes from the Anglo-Saxon word for a barrel.)

The growth of Carnival can be seen from the following figures:

Year	Number of ships	Combined tonnage
1972	1	27,284
1978	3	92,709
1994	9	496,893
2001	16	1,128,567

plus 3 being built with a combined tonnage of 304,000.

Thus by 2001 Carnival operated over one million GRT of cruise ships in its own name but the Carnival Corporation is actually much larger, as will be shown later.

Of the 16 ships in service in 2001, eight are sisters, representing the largest bloc of sister ships built for the passenger trade since the Cunard A class of vessels of the 1920s. With imaginative interior designs by Joe Farcus, each of these ships is of 70,367 GRT. The scope of this investment is shown when compared to the *Titanic* which was only 46,000 GRT and the *QE2* (also owned by Carnival now) of 70,327 GRT. Cartwright and Baird (1999) calculated that the cost of a modern cruise ship was of the order of $5000 per tonne, thus a combined tonnage of 1.3 million (including vessels being built) represents an investment of $6,500mn.

Hypergrowth of this scale can only occur by ensuring that the product offered is exactly what the market wants. The Carnival operation is far removed from the stuffy world of dressing for dinner – a traditionalist view of cruising. Non-stop action, music and 24-hour casino action is the order of the day on Carnival. In this way the company has been able to attract a completely new customer base.

Carnival were the first company to undertake 12-month cruising in the Caribbean, other companies having relocated ships during the hurricane season. However, as hurricanes disrupt very few cruises, Carnival's gamble has paid off. By not having to relocate ships the company was able to build the *Carnival Destiny*, the first passenger ship too wide to fit through the Panama Canal. *Carnival Destiny* and her growing band of sisters (all at over 101,000 GRT) have now been joined by even bigger ships from the Princess Cruises and Royal Caribbean operations, the latter having the world's largest passenger ship at the moment.

By introducing ships that met the vacation needs of singles and younger couples and operating mainly in the Caribbean, Carnival was able to grow very rapidly.

In 1984 Carnival launched the largest cruise line advertising campaign ever undertaken. Costing $10mn, two different 30-second advertisements were shown 133 times over the US. In 1987 Carnival made its IPO (Initial Public Offering) becoming a public corporation.

Carnival Cruises took a bold step in 1998 when, responding to customer demand they made the *Paradise* a totally smoke-free ship, banning all smoking on board – a move that has been followed by other operators. In 1996 they offered a guarantee to their cruises allowing customers to leave the ship with a refund at the first port of call if they were not satisfied and by 2000 had introduced a cyber café to all the vessels in the Carnival brand fleet.

Horizontal expansion

The concept of horizontal integration and growth was covered in both Chapters 3 and 6 of this material.

The Carnival brand appeals to young US vacationers. But of the 9.5 million people who undertook a cruise in 1999, many were neither young nor from the US. The UK is the second largest market and the rest of Europe provides another major slice. Many of those who enjoy cruises are older in years and the Carnival brand would not suit them. One of the best-known brands catering for the more mature vacationer is Holland America Cruises. Its ships are all in the premium price range and the cruises are less destination intensive than Carnival (Carnival ships typically stop at six destinations in seven days). Holland America has a very loyal customer base with high repeat business rates.

In 1987 Holland America acquired a 50 percent stake in Windstar Cruises (a company operating large sail-driven cruise ships) and completed the purchase the following year. Later in 1988, however, Carnival acquired Holland America giving it a foothold in the premier cruise market for more mature customers. Carnival changed very little. The appearance of Holland America ships, especially the livery, remained unchanged and they continued under their Dutch names with little reference to the new ownership.

In 1991 Carnival acquired a 25 percent stake in the luxury operator Seabourn Cruises (operator of a series of small yacht-like vessels). In 1996 Carnival purchased a 29.6 percent stake in the UK vacation business of Airtours plc at a cost of $310mn. Airtours were a very new entrant into the UK cruise market with an operation geared to the budget end of the market and linked to their core flights plus hotel package holidays. Spending another $300mn in 1997, Carnival bought Costa Cruises of Italy, a major player in both the US and European standard cruise markets. Carnival also added one of the Club Med sailing cruise vessels to the Windstar fleet.

In the early years of the twentieth century the UK government had kept Cunard (owners of some of the greatest Atlantic liners) out of the grasp of J P Morgan by providing subsidies on the stipulation that Cunard remained British. This changed in 1998 when Carnival acquired the Cunard cruise operation (including the *QE2*).

Thus by 1998, the Carnival Corporation had the following brands:

Carnival Cruises	US	Standard
Cunard	US/UK	Luxury
Costa	US/Europe	Standard
Airtours	UK	Standard
Seabourn	US	Luxury
Windstar	US	Niche sail cruises
America	US	Premier

Naturally not every customer is from the US or the UK but the market represents the majority.

By 2001 the acquisitions had added 33 ships plus 4 being built with a combined tonnage of 1,492,000 GRT, giving the Carnival Group 44 ships totaling well over 2 million GRT. This makes the Carnival Group easily the largest cruise conglomerate in the world with well over 33 percent of the global market – a market that is still growing.

Carnival has expanded by acquiring traditional brands and keeping them very much as is. Indeed it is doubtful whether the customer knows they are actually on a Carnival-owned vessel.

The cruise industry, like other multi-segment industries has a number of distinct customer bases. There are cruises for those on a budget and others that are extremely luxurious – the difference is price. There are also those such as the main Carnival operation that are for younger vacationers and others for those of more mature years. By building their own brand and acquiring others Carnival has been able to achieve hypergrowth in an industry where building times are relatively long and where the capital investment required is huge.

It has not all been a success. Carnival has tried to acquire other operators – Premier Cruises and Royal Caribbean – but without success. Their Latin America operation and another in the Far East were unsuccessful but it would be a brave person who placed a bet that Carnival will not re-enter these markets.

There is an excellent account of the Carnival operation in *Selling the Sea* (1997) by Bob Dickinson (now President of Carnival Cruises) and Andy Vladimir.

Fig. 7.1 shows a timeline for the Carnival Corporation.

CARNIVAL CRUISES: KEY INSIGHTS

» Carnival (and Arison) were not put off by initial problems.
» Listening to potential customers provided access to a new market segment.
» Carnival achieved growth by acquisition.
» Acquisitions kept their identity and thus their brand image and customer base.

» Starting small provided profits for expansion and allowed Carnival to build up a modern fleet.
» Eight vessels of a single class bring considerable economies of scale.
» Growth has been into different but linked segments and markets.

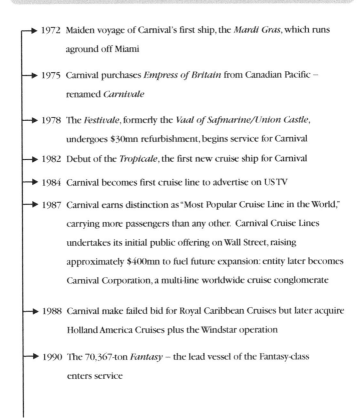

1972 Maiden voyage of Carnival's first ship, the *Mardi Gras*, which runs aground off Miami

1975 Carnival purchases *Empress of Britain* from Canadian Pacific – renamed *Carnivale*

1978 The *Festivale*, formerly the *Vaal of Safmarine/Union Castle*, undergoes $30mn refurbishment, begins service for Carnival

1982 Debut of the *Tropicale*, the first new cruise ship for Carnival

1984 Carnival becomes first cruise line to advertise on US TV

1987 Carnival earns distinction as "Most Popular Cruise Line in the World," carrying more passengers than any other. Carnival Cruise Lines undertakes its initial public offering on Wall Street, raising approximately $400mn to fuel future expansion: entity later becomes Carnival Corporation, a multi-line worldwide cruise conglomerate

1988 Carnival make failed bid for Royal Caribbean Cruises but later acquire Holland America Cruises plus the Windstar operation

1990 The 70,367-ton *Fantasy* – the lead vessel of the Fantasy-class enters service

Fig. 7.1

1991 Carnival acquires stake in Seabourn. Failed bid for stake in Premier Cruises

1993 Carnival set up Fiesta Marina Cruises for the Latin America market

1994 Carnival's parent company renamed Carnival Corporation to distinguish between it and its flagship brand, Carnival Cruise Lines. Fiesta Marina operation ceases

1996 *Carnival Destiny* enters service – the first passenger vessel to exceed 100,000. Carnival acquire 29.6% share of UK vacation and cruise operator Airtours. Vacation guarantee offered on Carnival brand

1997 Carnival and Airtours acquire Costa Cruises

1998 The eighth and last in the "Fantasy-class" series, the *Paradise*, enters service as the world's first totally non-smoking major cruise ship. Carnival acquires Cunard.

2001 Carnival introduces a brand new class of vessel with the launch of the 86,000-ton *Carnival Spirit* for the Alaska and Hawaii markets

Fig. 7.1 *(continued)*.

CASE 2: AIRBUS INDUSTRIE

Airbus, the first truly European company, is one of only two aircraft manufacturers in the global market for large commercial airliners. Airbus has experienced dramatic hypergrowth moving from zero sales in 1970 to being at the very top of the industry by 2000, having destroyed the almost monopoly position of the US in supply airframes outside the old Soviet sphere of influence.

Airbus was set up to design, build, sell, and support commercial aircraft with a capacity of 100 seats or more. Airbus does not supply the private flying, commuter or military markets.

The European commercial aircraft industry had been highly fragmented and nationalistic in the years immediately following the Second World War. In the UK, Vickers, Armstrong Whitworth, De Haviland, Handley Page, and Bristol were competing not only among themselves but also with Fokker in the Netherlands and Sud-Aviation in France. In the US, the start of the jet age saw Boeing, Douglas, Convair, and Lockheed as the main players.

Boeing, despite their success with large military aircraft such as the B17 Flying Fortress and the B29 Superfortress, had been less successful in the commercial market, with airlines claiming that Boeing did not listen to their requirements carefully enough and seemed content to offer re-workings of military transports, whereas Douglas built the airframes that the airlines wanted.

The British tried to break the stranglehold by introducing the first jet airliner, the Comet, to commercial service in 1952. Unfortunately the Comet carried too few passengers, was too slow, had too short a range, and worst of all had a fatal flaw in that the pressurization required to maintain life at 30,000 feet led to metal fatigue and the loss of two aircraft, together with their crews and passengers, in quick succession.

Boeing came to dominate the jet airliner market with Douglas (also in the US) in second place. The success of both companies was in offering a family of aircraft rather than a one-off product. Douglas ran into financial problems in the 1960s and were taken over by McDonnell to become McDonnell Douglas and were eventually acquired by Boeing in the 1990s. Lockheed with just one airliner product, the L1011 Tristar, could not compete.

The world market for airlines is sufficient for two large companies. For a time it looked as though these would be Boeing and McDonnell Douglas. However, the Europeans were about to re-enter the market in a spectacular manner.

The UK had merged two of the main manufacturers into the British Aircraft Corporation (BAC), now British Aerospace, in 1959 and still possessed one of the world's leading engine manufacturers, Rolls Royce. BAC produced the successful 1-11, a short-range twin-engined aircraft of which 252 were sold including 22 assembled in Romania. The French Sud Est concern had developed the highly successful Caravelle, selling 282 between 1955 and 1973. Sud Est became part of

Aerospatiale and that concern, together with BAC, had responsibility for the development of the Anglo-French supersonic jet transport, Concorde.

Try as they might, the Europeans could not break the hegemony of the US manufactures. Dassault, another French manufacture, famed for its military aircraft including the Mirage, designed and built the twin-engined Mercure in the early 1970s but only sold ten. It was important for the European nations not to be left out as they needed the designers and the expertise for military aircraft or else they would be dependent on the US for both military and civilian designs.

By 1970, Boeing had developed a complete family of aircraft. Building on the success of the 707, they had introduced or were developing the medium range 727, the short range 737 (currently the best-selling jet airliner ever) the huge 747 Jumbo and the 757 replacement for the 727 and the wide-bodied 767. The latter two aircraft had identical controls so that crew trained on one could switch to the other with the minimum of difficulty.

On December 18, 1970 a new organization was founded as a *groupement d'intérêt économique* (GIE) in France. The organization was Airbus Industrie. The organization possessed no aircraft, no designs, few staff and no plant. Its chairman, Henri Zeigler, had been a hero of the French Resistance during the war and believed that, working together, Europeans could once more become a force in the aircraft industry.

A GIE was a device developed in France to assist winegrowers, whereby a group pools resources and capital, with the assets and profits appearing on the books of the individual members. A GIE pays no tax (although the members do).

The idea of a joint French–UK–German consortium had been gathering momentum since 1965 when talks had been held between the UK and France. By 1967 provisional agreement had been made to build a twin-engined jet with the UK and France providing 37.5 percent of the required development cost of $320mn and Germany providing the remaining 20 percent. Rolls Royce would supply the engines, with 75 percent of their development costs being met by the UK government and the rest by France and Germany. The aircraft was to enter service in 1973.

In 1969, due to financial pressures, the UK withdrew from the project. Hawker Siddeley, the other main UK manufacturer, had already completed most of the design work on the wing for the new aircraft. The wing is one of the most critical areas of aircraft design dictating as it does the whole performance envelope. As a result of German negotiations to keep the expertise of UK designers within the project although the UK was out of the project, Hawker Siddeley were contracted to design and build the wings.

The concept of a wide-bodied, twin-engined aircraft had been put forward by Frank Kolk of American Airlines as the ideal product for the lucrative twin-city pairs (Chicago–New York, Miami–Atlanta etc.) market in the US. However, Boeing preferred to develop their 747 Jumbo, an aircraft that was too large for such routes, and Douglas and Lockheed were reluctant to have less than three engines on their new developments, the DC10 and L-1011 Tristar, respectively – the market for Airbus Industrie looked wide open. The new fan jet engines that powered the 747, DC10 and Tristar were far more powerful and reliable than earlier jet engines and Airbus felt confident that two engines would be sufficient for a wide-bodied aircraft, a confidence not felt at the time in the US.

The other problem the CEO of Airbus, Roger Beteille, knew the organization faced was a reluctance of the US airlines to buy a foreign product. While sales in the rest of the world are important, the US market is the key one. If Airbus was to become a global player it would need to compete with the US manufacturers head to head – for a history of the rivalry between Boeing and Airbus, see Lynn (1995).

In 1976, in their study of the crash of a DC10 outside Paris, Paul Eddy and his colleagues from the *Sunday Times* Insight Team of investigative journalists, commented on the complete domination of the market by US companies and went on to state that the existence of Airbus proved their case, as Airbus had only made 30 sales of their first product, the A300, to "captive" national French and German airlines.

Beteille wanted to strengthen and deepen the consortium; Lynn reports that there were even talks with Boeing. He was able to involve the Italians and the Dutch in the consortium. This was important because it meant that four of the most influential European Economic Community (EEC, now the European Union, EU) members were part of Airbus and this might make national airlines in the Netherlands and Italy more likely to consider the A300. Interestingly the *lingua franca* for Airbus was to be English – perhaps a reflection of US influence over the industry.

The testing of the A300 went well, but as commented above, sales were hard to come by. In 1977, Airbus had not sold a single aircraft to a US airline, but nevertheless set up an office in New York. George Ward, vice president of the US operation, brokered a deal with Eastern Airlines whereby Eastern would be supplied with some A300s to try out. If the trials went well Eastern could then buy the aircraft. Airbus had to meet the maintenance and certification costs. The trials did go well, Eastern buying 23 A300s with options on 9 more and options for 25 of the next model – a deal worth $778mn. As Eastern was short of cash, Airbus assisted with the financing. The economic sense of selling to a customer who is so short of cash that they cannot pay may seem strange but the marketing sense of A300s in the livery of a US airline and operating out of US airports is easy to comprehend. Not surprisingly both Boeing and McDonnell Douglas (Douglas had been taken over by then) complained about the financing arrangements – the first of many complaints about the degree to which European governments subsidized Airbus. It has to be said, however, that the engines were from the US and together with US manufactured components for the airframe made up 25 percent of the cost – thus helping US firms and jobs.

Boeing fought back with the narrow-bodied 757 and the wide-bodied 767, both aircraft that have been very popular. Boeing courted the UK for a collaborative arrangement (British Airways was a major Boeing customer – actually the launch customer for the 757) but in 1978 the UK rejoined the Airbus consortium in time for the announcement of the next model, a smaller derivative of the A300, the A310. Between 1970 and 1978 Airbus had only sold 38 aircraft but by the end of 1979 orders stood at 256, representing no fewer than 32 different customers and giving Airbus a 26 percent share of the world market.

Airbus developed a type of domino sales technique, selling to adjacent countries one after the other in a line stretching from the Mediterranean to Japan. Lynn called this "the Silk Route Strategy".

In 1981 Airbus announced a direct competitor to the smaller Boeing 737 and McDonnell Douglas DC9, the new model to be called the

A320. It was to be the first fly-by-wire aircraft, relying on computers to activate the control hydraulics.

By 1984 when Pan Am bought 28 A300s, Airbus was an established name in the industry and the next year the A300/310 gained 44.5 percent of the wide-body market with McDonnell Douglas having a mere 2.5 percent. Boeing might still be the biggest name but only just.

The next member of the Airbus family broke new ground in aviation. Virtually the same long-range aircraft can be supplied with two engines as an A330 or four engines as an A340. This gives considerable flexibility for Airbus to offer different ranges and payloads using very similar jigs.

That the US manufacturer (by the millennium this was just Boeing) were worried was shown by the repeated complaints to the General Agreement on Tariff and Trade talks and the World Trade Organization that came out of GATT in the 1990s. The US contention is that Airbus is subsidized to an unfair degree and uses political influence to sell aircraft. The Europeans respond that Boeing is heavily subsidized through its military contracts. There are plenty of examples of US politicians lobbying for sales so it may well be a case of six of one and half a dozen of the other.

With its Central Office in Toulouse, France, Airbus boasts the most modern and comprehensive airliner family in the world and now captures about half of all commercial airliner orders. By 2001, more than 2500 Airbus aircraft were in operation with 186 airlines in all regions of the globe. In 2000, the turnover of Airbus was $17.2bn and had booked more than 4300 orders by the end of June 2001. The company actually produces more than one aircraft every working day and this rate keeps increasing.

Now established as a French simplified joint stock company (Société par Actions Simplifiée, SAS), Airbus directly employs some 44,000 people in 16 different sites in Europe.

Growth philosophy

In order to grow, Airbus Industrie has adopted the philosophy of *anticipating the market*, offering *innovation* and greater value, focusing on *passenger comfort*, and creating a *true family* of aircraft. It is only with the family of aircraft that Airbus has been able to challenge the Boeing hegemony – in effect playing Boeing at their own game.

The current structure of Airbus

On July 11, 2001, Airbus formally became a single integrated company, with retroactive effect from January 1, 2001, thus passing another major milestone in its history of achievements since its creation as a consortium in 1970.

All Airbus resources and know-how located in France, Germany, Spain and the UK have now been consolidated into a single standard operating company, under the day-to-day control of a single management team.

The integration of all its functions should enable Airbus to obtain even greater efficiency through the concentration of purchasing power, faster decision making, and a direct control over costs. Synergies thus generated are expected to reach at least euro350mn per annum by 2004.

The two shareholders, the European Aeronautic Defence and Space Company (EADS) and BAE Systems of the UK, respectively hold 80 percent and 20 percent of the new stock in the revised company.

How the growth has come about

The remarkable growth of Airbus has come about because the company understood that the only way to compete effectively was to listen to the market and then respond to its demands. Boeing were criticized at one time for not listening to their customers and, according to Karl Sabbach, it was only with the development of their competitor to the A330/340, the Boeing 777, that they became truly responsive to the market. As a result of Airbus spending considerable time listening to customers and potential customers, the original aircraft, the A300, is now the first of a family of jetliners, each one of which has been built for a particular market niche, from short to ultra-long haul.

In addition, each aircraft shares many characteristics with the others, bringing obvious benefits to pilots, crews and maintenance staff as well as to the profit and loss account of airlines, thanks to reduced training and maintenance costs.

The A380 program for a very large aircraft (larger than the current Boeing 747 models), launched in December 2000, is the latest and most striking example of this approach. Some 20 major airlines, some 50 airports as well as international airworthiness authorities, suppliers and subcontractors, all collaborated on the development of this aircraft from day one. This ensures that the A380 will satisfy airline, passenger, infrastructure, and environmental demands well into the twenty-first century.

Some of the Airbus innovations have been truly revolutionary in the airline industry. Others are incremental but have helped provide a significant competitive edge. One of the best examples is the introduction of the first fly-by-wire system in the A320 in 1988. This resulted not only in more precision, greater ergonomics and easier operation but also in cockpit commonality across the entire fly-by-wire aircraft family. Fly-by-wire has since become an industry standard, as have twin engines for longer flights – a concept pioneered in the A300.

The pioneers who started Airbus had vision and saw that the European aircraft industry might be moribund, but that working together could revive it. They looked at the market and saw that existing manufacturers had not listened to either the passengers' or the operators' demands. There was a niche to be filled: a short- to medium-range aircraft that had the operating economics of a twin-engined aircraft and the ability to carry 250–300 passengers in comfort.

The industry will never be the same again

Because no single European manufacturer had the resources to overcome the US giants, it was clear that European aircraft manufacturers would have to cooperate to beat a common rival. Thus the former Airbus consortium was created. By overcoming national divides, sharing development costs, collaborating in the interests of a greater market share, and even agreeing a common set of measurements and a common language, Airbus has been able to grow from nothing in the late 1960s to joint number 1 by the millennium.

When the four-engined A340 entered service in 1993, it was the first entirely new, long-haul aircraft to start commercial operations for more than 20 years. The twin-engined A330 which joined it a year later combined some of the lowest operating costs of any aircraft ever designed with maximum flexibility for a wide range of route structures. The next development, the A380, will be capable of transporting 555 passengers over distances of up to 14,800km (8000nm). Its freight version will carry 150 tonnes (331,000lbs) over 10,410km (5620nm).

The A380 superjumbo will provide 15–20 percent lower operating costs, 10–15 percent more range, lower fuel burn, less noise and lower emissions than the largest aircraft flying today. While offering all the advantages of an all-new design, it will extend the benefits of Airbus commonality into the very large aircraft sector, enabling pilots to transition from other Airbus aircraft to the A380 with only minor additional training.

The Airbus family of products

A300	250 seats	2 engines	wide body	
A310	218 seats	2 engines	wide body	
A319	120 seats	2 engines	wide body	
A320	130–170 seats	2 engines	narrow body	
A321	180–200 seats	2 engines	narrow body	
A330	335–340 seats	2 engines	narrow body	
A340	375–440 seats	4 engines	wide body	long range
A380	555 seats	4 engines	wide body	long range

Fig. 7.2 shows a timeline for Airbus Industrie.

AIRBUS INDUSTRIE: KEY INSIGHTS

The hypergrowth of Airbus Industrie has been all the more remarkable because of the need to start from scratch in an industry where credibility is built up over years and where customers have very long-term relationships with their suppliers. The success of Airbus can be attributed to:

» Building on previous national reputations in the industry.
» Combining national strengths.
» Imaginative financing arrangements.
» Careful listening to customers.
» High build quality.
» Providing a family of products.
» Aggressive marketing.

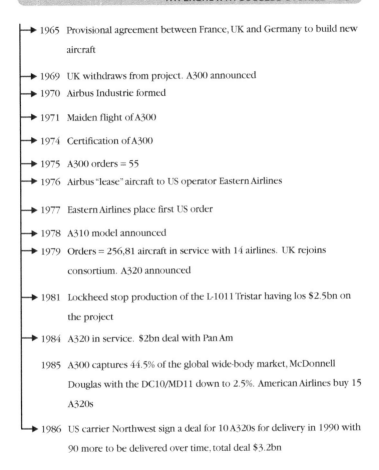

1965   Provisional agreement between France, UK and Germany to build new aircraft

1969   UK withdraws from project. A300 announced

1970   Airbus Industrie formed

1971   Maiden flight of A300

1974   Certification of A300

1975   A300 orders = 55

1976   Airbus "lease" aircraft to US operator Eastern Airlines

1977   Eastern Airlines place first US order

1978   A310 model announced

1979   Orders = 256, 81 aircraft in service with 14 airlines. UK rejoins consortium. A320 announced

1981   Lockheed stop production of the L-1011 Tristar having los $2.5bn on the project

1984   A320 in service. $2bn deal with Pan Am

1985   A300 captures 44.5% of the global wide-body market, McDonnell Douglas with the DC10/MD11 down to 2.5%. American Airlines buy 15 A320s

1986   US carrier Northwest sign a deal for 10 A320s for delivery in 1990 with 90 more to be delivered over time, total deal $3.2bn

Fig. 7.2

1987   Airbus replace Boeing as market leader in the wide-body sector with 47.9%

1989   A321 added to range

1991   United Airlines order 50 aircraft plus options on 50 more in a $3bn deal

1992   A319 added to range

1993   A340 – long-haul aircraft added to range. GATT negotiations end formal US threat of sanctions over Airbus

1994   A330 added to range. Airbus gain 30% of total world civil aerospace industry

1999   A380 very large aircraft announced

Fig. 7.2   *(continued)*.

» A willingness to build business.
» Putting huge efforts into penetrating the main market – the US.

CASE 3: SAMSUNG ELECTRONICS

In the early 1950s, South Korea was ravaged by what the United Nations called a police action but what was, in all respects, a full-blown war against South Korea. From 1950 until 1952 the US, the UK and a host of UN members fought to stem the tide of a North Korean and eventual Chinese invasion across the 48th Parallel, the dividing line between North and South Korea. For much of the rest of the twentieth century, an uneasy truce existed on the Korean Peninsular with occasional incursions and raids.

The Korean people, however, possess stamina. From the ravages of war, South Korea has become one of the powerhouses of the Asian economic boom. Homes, roads, and ports throughout the world see Korean electronics, Korean automobiles and Korean-built ships in increasing numbers – goods that are not only competitive but of high quality.

Samsung is now a well-known name in the consumer electronics market throughout the world and yet the company was only formed in 1969, and has thus seen massive growth.

In 1970, the first product was (by twenty-first-century standards), a primitive black and white television set. While television was by then an integral part of North American and European daily life there were still vast parts of the world where it was new, and low cost sets were much valued. By 1971 Samsung were exporting their sets to Panama, a useful gateway to Central and South America. The Korean home market for sets was also developing and Samsung were in a good position to take advantage of this.

A sensible expansion was from brown goods into white goods, thus catering for similar markets with different products. In 1974 the company began to manufacture refrigerators and then later that year, washing machines. By 1976 they had produced their one millionth black and white TV set and were developing a 35.5cm (14in.) color model, the first of which were exported (again to Panama) in 1977. By 1978 the number of black and white TV sets produced reached 4 million, with the market showing no sign of decline despite the growth in the use of color sets.

Microwave technology for domestic applications was then just coming into vogue and Samsung began mass production of microwave ovens in 1979. The company was still staying within the domestic brown/white goods market but expanding its range and types of product. Air conditioners were developed in 1980 and by 1981 the 10 millionth black and white TV set had been produced with production of color sets topping one million the next year.

For an organization in a country such as Korea, exports are a necessity. The first microwave exports were to Canada in 1981 with color TVs being exported to Japan in 1982. In that same year Samsung made its first manufacturing moves outside Korea by opening a plant in Portugal and establishing a sales subsidiary in West Germany, thus giving it a presence in Europe.

The early 1980s saw the beginnings of a revolution in business machinery with the introduction of the personal computer (PC). Many of the original companies in this market have been subsumed by competitors but Samsung, which started manufacture of PCs in 1983, is still a major producer. From a situation where few in the world had seen a computer in 1970, by 2000 most people in the developed world have a PC at work and another in their home. The market is nearly as large as that for TV sets.

The Portuguese factory began exporting color TVs in 1983 and the following year a UK sales subsidiary was formed, together with the company's first plant in the US. Samsung also began the export of the latest piece of brown goods technology to become popular, the videocassette recorder (VCR). The manufacture of VCRs was a natural progression from TVs, just as the move into camcorders was a natural development from VCR production.

By 1986, the sales of black and white TVs had declined but the company produced their 10 millionth color set, production of these and microwaves also taking place in a new plant in the UK. The years 1986-9 were ones of considerable growth for Samsung despite a world recession that was beginning to bite. Sales subsidiaries/joint ventures were established in Australia, Canada, and France with new plants in Thailand, Malaysia, and Mexico plus research establishments in the US and Japan. By 1989 the production of color TVs had doubled from 1986 and stood at 20 million.

1990 saw the introduction of notebook computers to the product range and the development of the latest business technology product (and soon to storm the domestic market), the mobile telephone.

The fall of the Berlin Wall and the collapse of communism led to the development of a plant in what is now the Czech Republic in 1992 and a VCR production joint venture in China. By 1992, Samsung had become the first Korean manufacturer to achieve exports of $40bn.

During the 1990s Samsung continued to develop its product range especially for the mobile telephone, computer and home entertainment markets. Samsung cameras and camcorders joined the product range and the company was well placed to take advantage of the developments in digital photography brought about by the synergy between computer and camera technology.

The Samsung philosophy

While Samsung's growth has been extremely rapid, it has clearly followed a pattern of synergy developments.

Black and white televisions led naturally to color models and the building of a brand base in the domestic products market (brown good sector). People in the market for a TV are also likely to purchase a refrigerator, a washing machine and a microwave oven. If they were delighted with their Samsung TV, might they not want other Samsung domestic products? Computer developments follow on from TVs and Samsung's move into other forms of office machinery, facsimile machines etc. is a natural development. This form of connected growth coupled with the development of plants in their main markets has been a considerable factor in the success of the company.

Social attitudes

Samsung Electronics' main priorities are that of any commercial organization – a commitment to the customer and shareholder. Samsung Electronics' business philosophy stresses providing the products that customers need, judging them from the customers' point of view, and satisfying customers with advanced technology and services. Under the corporate motto "creating new lifestyles for the world," Samsung Electronics strives to create a brighter future for people.

With regard to the shareholders, Samsung Electronics is committed to maximizing profits. To achieve this, Samsung is continuously working to expand its position as a global company through high profits, maintaining a healthy financial structure and balancing its business structure. Samsung has positioned into four main business units – Home Network, Office Network, Mobile Network, and core component Businesses. The company is global in nature although still retains a Korean philosophy. With 25 worldwide production bases and 59 sales subsidiaries in 46 countries, the company has a brand that is recognized on all continents.

Samsung Electronics is definitely not satisfied with simply producing and selling products. The company wishes to be regarded as an international corporate citizen by transferring technology and know-how to seven operations overseas, providing stable employment and increasing the number of parts produced locally. This is an important facet of the philosophy especially as customers become more concerned about those who manufacture products, as discussed in Chapter 5.

Samsung Electronics believes that it is socially responsible and has a healthy future-oriented corporate culture. All employees are encouraged to achieve their best in a work environment that is unrestricted and creative. Moreover, the company is committed to protecting the environment, supporting cultural activities, and promoting various community service programs.

In common with other far-eastern companies, Samsung believes in making life more convenient, building a more prosperous future and promoting social harmony with abundant opportunities. Thus, Samsung state that the company is continuously searching for ways to transform the world for a better tomorrow.

For the past half-century, Samsung employees have been guided by a corporate philosophy that states, ''We will devote our people and technology to create superior products and services, thereby contributing to a better global society.'' Today this corporate philosophy unites all Samsung-affiliated companies.

To continue to grow, Samsung have a need for the best people available – people who are technically skilled, socially adept, comfortable in other cultures, confident, creative, studious, and focused on the future. Samsung aims to attract and nurture the best talents, and to foster a corporate culture in which they can thrive. Only then, the company believes, can customer satisfaction and sustainable corporate growth be assured.

The mindset of contributing to society through social development while pursuing business activities is deeply ingrained in Samsung's corporate culture. Senior management believes that social commitment is their duty as human beings.

On their Website (see Chapter 9), Samsung state:

''Numerous new businesses and products are being developed in the wake of digital convergence and the survival or non survival of a company can be determined in 2 or 3 months due to the fast changes that are taking place. We have entered the age of oligopoly

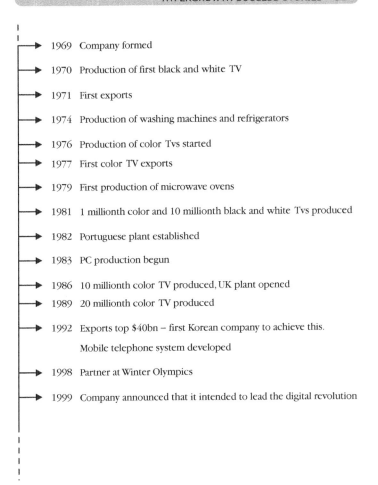

1969   Company formed

1970   Production of first black and white TV

1971   First exports

1974   Production of washing machines and refrigerators

1976   Production of color Tvs started

1977   First color TV exports

1979   First production of microwave ovens

1981   1 millionth color and 10 millionth black and white Tvs produced

1982   Portuguese plant established

1983   PC production begun

1986   10 millionth color TV produced, UK plant opened

1989   20 millionth color TV produced

1992   Exports top $40bn – first Korean company to achieve this.
Mobile telephone system developed

1998   Partner at Winter Olympics

1999   Company announced that it intended to lead the digital revolution

Fig. 7.3

where only a few companies can survive due to the reduction in product life cycle and market opening. Unlike the past when 'cheap and fast' production was key to success, we must equip ourselves with other strengths such as brand power, logistics, intellectual property and core competencies to set ourselves apart from other companies."

The digital electronics era, of which we are just at the start, will be centered on digital and network technology where everything will be integrated with not only synergies of technology but also synergies between technology and services. Numerous new businesses will be generated as electrical appliances and services merge with each other. Therefore, it is important for companies such as Samsung to have the relevant capabilities and technologies and the ability to use them in an integrated way. In that direction lies growth. In 2001 Samsung announced the first mobile video telephone, showing that they were still at the very cutting edge of technology.

Fig. 7.3 shows a timeline for Samsung.

SAMSUNG: KEY INSIGHTS

» Growth has been rapid but not random.
» Product developments have led on naturally from each other.
» Plants have been set up in major areas of sales.
» Quality is part of the philosophy of the company.
» Samsung has a social conscience and this dictates the way the company interfaces with customers and employees.
» The company have always been ready to take advantage of the next technological advance.

Key Concepts and Thinkers

Get to grips with the lexicon of hypergrowth through the *ExpressExec* hypergrowth glossary in this chapter, which also covers:

» key concepts;
» key thinkers.

A GLOSSARY FOR HYPERGROWTH

Acquisitions

The process of growing by gaining an ownership interest in another company. Acquisition can be for the purpose of removing a competitor or diversifying either into a different region or area, or a new field of operation. One of the major advantages of growing by acquisition is that the acquired company may well have a loyal customer base that, with careful retention of brands etc., can be retained. A disadvantage is that employees who may be used to a different organizational culture will need to be absorbed. Companies are often vulnerable to acquisition at the *adolescence*, *rejuvenation* or *decline* stages of the organizational life cycle (see below), as they often need injections of cash at these times.

Alliances

Agreements between companies to cooperate in certain areas for mutual benefit. The advantage to a growing company is that they can gain experience in a market without having to set up a full-scale operation. They will, however, be required to share some of their proprietary knowledge with their partners who may later become competitors. The issue of balance is a delicate one and the whole situation needs careful analysis before such alliances are undertaken.

Business plan

The plan, often financial, that details how the company intends to grow in the short to medium term. Business planning is an important area of managerial activity as the business plan will be the basis for approaches to banks and investors for cash to fund growth. There is an *ExpressExec* title directly concerned with the business plan.

Culture

The values, attitudes, and beliefs ascribed to and accepted by a group, nation or organization. In effect, "the way we do things around here."

Diversification

A growth mechanism that involves expanding the portfolio of products/services offered either organically or by acquiring other companies.

Horizontal diversification involves expanding into linked products/ services, e.g. from TVs to video recorders to hi-fi systems etc. Vertical diversification is the acquisition of other parts of the value chain. Many vacation companies grow by moving from offering holidays to acquiring airline interests thus enabling them to offer an airport–resort service to their customers.

Export processing zones (EPZs)

Areas set up by governments (often in the developing world) where raw materials are imported and finished products manufactured and exported free of any customs duties.

Foreign direct investment (FDI)

The process whereby foreign companies either set up operations abroad or buy local companies and integrate them into their operations.

Globalization

The integration of the global economy by the dismantling of trade and political barriers and the increasing political and economic power of multinational corporations.

Global operation

This refers to an organization that operates on a worldwide basis and yet is integrated into the local community and economy.

Internet-specific companies

These are companies set up specifically to exploit the capabilities of the Internet. They fall into two categories. First, there are those companies that are using the Internet as their prime method of trading (e-commerce) of which Amazon.com is one of the best known examples. The second category is companies that provide an Internet service, and this includes the ISPs and search engine providers (see later) and companies such as Cisco. Christopher Price (see under key thinkers) has profiled many of those who have developed companies in this area and a number of the *Business the XXX Way* books from Capstone (listed in Chapter 9) cover the growth of companies related to Internet activities.

Joint ventures

Temporary alliances (see earlier) where two or more companies agree to work on specific projects in partnership. Often used when companies from different countries wish to work together.

Mergers

Technically different from an acquisition where one company purchases another, in a merger two or more companies come together to form a new entity.

North American Free Trade Agreement (NAFTA)

A free trade agreement between the US, Canada, and Mexico.

Organizational life cycle

Similar to the human or product life cycles, the organizational life cycle represents the stages an organization passes through. Those stages are birth, adolescence, maturity, menopause, and either rejuvenation or decline. Growth is most likely to occur at the birth, adolescence or rejuvenation stages. Organizations in adolescence or decline are vulnerable to acquisition by other organizations seeking to grow as it is at these times that an organization may be in urgent need of cash.

Strategic alliance

Cooperation between companies, often across national borders. Such alliances may take the form of joint ventures and projects, but are mergers as each partner retains its independent identity.

KEY THINKERS

All of the books referred to in this section are listed fully in Chapter 9.

Anslinger, Patricia L.

A co-worker with Thomas Copeland (see below), Anslinger is a principle of the McKinsey & Company New York office. As one of the world's premier consulting firms, McKinsey was responsible for commissioning the research that led to Tom Peters and Bob Waterman writing *In Search of Excellence* – still one of the best selling business books of all time. Anslinger, together with Copeland, writing in the Harvard Business Review text, *Strategies for Growth*, has challenged the perceived wisdom that acquisitions should be based on synergy. They have provided evidence that with care, even nonsynergical acquisitions can make a large and swift contribution to a company's bottom line.

Anslinger has contributed to the *Harvard Business Review*, *McKinsey Quarterly* and *Director and Boards*.

» Books: ''Growth through Acquisitions'' (with Copeland T) in Harvard Business Review, *Strategies for Growth* (1994).

Baghai, Mehrdad

Together with Stephen Coley and David White, Baghai Mehrdad wrote *The Alchemy of Growth* while at McKinsey & Company (cf. Anslinger and Copeland).

While the word ''alchemy'' might suggest that growth is a mystical quality, the study of 30 companies provides a practical guide combined with an in-depth understanding of the growth process. The all-important processes of laying foundations and proactively seeking out opportunities show that there is nothing magical about growth – it stems from hard work.

The authors make the point that growth cannot always be continued. One of the complaints that has been made about the ideas of Tom Peters and Bob Waterman (also from McKinsey) in *In Search of Excellence* has been that companies that were doing well in the late 1970s and early 1980s had faltered later on. Baghai et al. recognize that since writing *The Alchemy of Growth* in 1999, some of the companies studied have not been as successful in growing as they had been. That does not detract from the lessons that can be learnt. Growth is a function of the present with an anticipation of the future. Sometimes the future can be predicted but in many cases it cannot be – except by hindsight. Growth can be slow for reasons totally unconnected with the company. A well-managed company will, however, have the reserves to weather a slump and be ready to grow again when the circumstances are right.

» Books: *The Alchemy of Growth* with Stephen Coley and David White (1999).

Coley, Stephen

See Baghai, Mehrdad above.

» Books: *The Alchemy of Growth* with Mehrdad Baghai and David White (1999).

Copeland, Thomas

A co-worker of Anslinger (see above), Copeland was a professor of finance at UCLA before becoming director of financial services at the consulting firm of McKinsey & Company in New York. Of particular interest in the context of this material is his work with Anslinger on the benefits of nonsynergical growth and the links between finance and policy as described in his 1988 text, *Financial Theory and Corporate Policy*.

» Books: *Financial Theory and Corporate Policy* (1988).
   "Growth through Acquisitions" (with Anslinger P) in Harvard Business Review, *Strategies for Growth* (1994).

Giddens, A.

Anthony Giddens is the director of the London School of Economics and the pioneer of the "Third Way" concept between left and right wing that has been adopted by the UK prime minister, Tony Blair. In 1999 he was asked to present the BBC Reith Lecture and did so on the implications of globalization and the world becoming more homogenous. Challenging in its views, the lecture has now been produced in book form and makes fascinating reading as Giddens looks not only at business but also at traditions and the family etc. He also provides a superb reading list. Frequently consulted by heads of state, Giddens has written a large number of books on political and social themes that are outside the scope of this material.

» Books: *Runaway World* (1999).

Hertz, Noreena

Associate director of the Centre for International Management at the Judge Institute of the University of Cambridge, UK, Hertz has recently (2001) written *The Silent Takeover* in which she argues that global capitalism could cause the death of the very democracy that has allowed it to flourish. While the title might appear as a contradiction as there are few corporate takeovers and mergers that are not reported widely in the media, the "takeover" Hertz refers to is of an altogether different order, referring to the takeover of the planet itself rather than a business rival and "silent" because few have realized that it may be happening. She points out that of the world's largest economies, 51 are now corporations and only 49 are nation-states. Hertz has produced a highly readable account of economic change over the past two decades, an account her style makes highly readable. Hertz's view of globalization is that not everyone benefits from the capitalist dream and that CEOs often have more power than elected leaders. Hertz sees a time in the not too distant future when it is consumers' wallets that will decide policy and not the ballot box.

Hypergrowth has produced larger and larger organizations of a global nature and Hertz's concern is that such hypergrowth may be producing organizations that are something more than just commercial entities and that while all organizations have a political and social agenda, in huge organizations these agendas may begin to supplant the commercial ones.

» Books: *Russian Business Relationships in the Wake of Reform* (1997).
    The Silent Takeover (2001).

Klein, Naomi

Naomi Klein is a Canadian journalist and commentator who has been especially concerned with the effects of branding and globalization on society. In her book, *No Logo* (shortlisted for the Guardian First Book Award in 2000) she explores the effects of EPZs (see above) on the economies of countries such as the Philippines and argues that there appears to be little benefit to workers in such areas. She also examines the power of the consumer to make large organizations accountable. While mainly considering US based multi-nations she also examines the behavior of Shell and other European operations. *No Logo* contains a useful reading list for those interested in studying how some hypergrowth organizations have dealt with issues of globalization. Klein believes that the manner of their growth may have been detrimental to the societies within which they operate, even if it has been profitable for managers and shareholders.

» Books: *No Logo* (2000)
» Magazine and journals: weekly column in the *Globe & Mail* (Canada)

Korten, David C.

The author of the best-selling *When Corporations Rule the World*, Korten addresses the issue of modern corporate power, exposing the harmful effects globalization is having not only on economics, but also on politics, society and the environment. His work documents the devastating consequences as corporations recreate values and institutions to serve their own and their stockholders' narrow financial interests. Korten outlines a strategy for creating localized economies that empower people and communities within a system of global cooperation. While his work is sometimes considered left-wing and controversial, Korten does attempt to put a model in place to remedy what he sees as the disastrous effects of globalization and he has certainly enlivened and informed the debate by bringing it to a larger and more popular audience.

In *The Post Corporate World* Korten examines the deep and growing gap between the promises of the new global capitalism and the reality of insecurity, inequality, social breakdown, spiritual emptiness, and environmental destruction he believes that it leaves in its wake. The book looks at what went wrong and why, drawing on insights from the new biology and a growing human understanding of living systems to propose a solution – an economy that takes market principles seriously but also reflects the creativity and uniqueness of the individual. Korten also suggests specific actions to free the creative powers of individuals and societies through the realization of real democracy, the local rooting of capital through stakeholder ownership, and a restructuring of the rules of commerce to create market economies that combine market principles with a culture that nurtures social bonding and responsibility. This book is a useful complement to his earlier work, *Globalizing Civil Society*.

» Books: *Getting to the 21st Century: Voluntary Action and the Global Agenda* (1990).
  When Corporations Rule the World (1995).
  Globalizing Civil Society (1997).
  The Post Corporate World (2000).

Lorange, Peter

Peter Lorange, president of IMD in Switzerland and formerly president of the Norwegian School of Management and a teacher at Wharton and MIT has contributed to the issue of growth through his work with Johan Roos on strategic alliances. Together they produced the classic text on alliance and joint ventures – *Strategic Alliances* (1992).

The number of such alliances grew rapidly throughout the last decade of the twentieth century, growth that seems set to continue into the twenty-first. By studying a large number of such operations, Lorange and Roos have been able to generate a blueprint for managing growth through this means. The point is made that the process is one that occurs over time and comprises steps that are commercial, analytical and political. Lorange and Roos stress the importance of trust in the relationships – not always the easiest task in a competitive environment.

» Books: *Strategic Alliances: Formation, Implementation and Evolution* with J. Roos (1992).
  The Strategic Planning Process (1994)

Means, Grady E.

Grady E. Means is global leader of the Strategy Consulting group of the Management Consulting Services (MCS) practice of Pricewaterhouse

Coopers. In this role he oversees a global organization that integrates a full range of consulting services – from business strategy development and operations to resource productivity and cost reduction and organizational restructuring to technology design – into a coherent package of solutions to help large companies succeed in today's New Economy.

Grady E. Means has been a business strategy consultant and adviser to top management and government leaders for nearly 30 years. During that time, he has managed projects for many companies in nearly all sectors of the economy, including manufacturing, telecommunications, entertainment, high technology, financial services (banking and insurance), healthcare, retail, utilities, and government. He served in the White House as assistant to vice president Nelson Rockefeller for domestic policy development and at the US Department of Health, Education and Welfare, where he was staff economist in the Office of the Secretary. He is a former staff member of the Graduate School of Business at Stanford University.

Means is frequently interviewed and quoted in national and international business media. He is co-author of the books, *Wisdom of CEOs*, and *MetaCapitalism: The E-Business Revolution and the Design of 21st Century Companies and Markets*.

In *MetaCapitalism*, written with David M. Schneider, Means provides a comprehensive analysis of how the Internet, combined with major improvements in business management, efficiency, and productivity in the 1990s is leading to a fundamental transformation of global business by creating unprecedented economic value and wealth and accelerating the growth of worldwide capital markets from $20trn to levels potentially approaching $200trn in less than 10 years.

Means and Schneider show how through the formation of e-markets, online exchanges and networked business communities, traditionally successful business models are turned on their heads with the transition towards decapitalization and external networks, rather than owning every aspect of production. *MetaCapitalism* describes how capital markets are increasingly rewarding companies that are using new technology to constantly reorganize themselves by integrating new players and forging new partnerships and alliances, rather than companies who continue to maintain a large internal capital base of manufacturing sites, distribution centers, and retail outlets.

They also show how modern growth leads to an increase in outsourcing thus providing a useful link to many of the writers on globalization.

In *Wisdom of CEOs*, Means and his associates have gathered together contributions from those running some of the best-known hypergrowth organizations and provide an analysis of recent changes to the way business is conducted and predictions for the future.

» Books: *Wisdom of CEOs* with W.G. Dauphinais, C. Price and G. Gardner (2000).

    MetaCapitalism: The E-Business Revolution and the Design of 21st Century Companies and Markets with D. Schneider (2000).

Meyer, Peter

President of the Meyer Consulting Group, Peter Meyer was for many years with IBM. A contributor of what he has termed "warp-speed" growth, an oblique reference to the popular *Star Trek* series of TV episodes and movies, Meyer stresses the importance of the three main resources for hypergrowth: people, time, and money. In his book, *Hypergrowth*, Meyer encourages managers to build up their vision of where the company is going as one would build up a jigsaw puzzle. While the complete picture may be visible straightaway, the more pieces there are in place, the clearer the way the puzzle will be completed becomes. Meyer stresses the importance of having the right people in place to support growth – without them growth may be slowed, indeed may be impossible.

» Books: *Warp-Speed Growth* (2000).

Porter, Michael

A renowned professor at Harvard Business School, Porter has been the world authority on competition and competitive strategies since the 1980s. His writing has informed those in both industry and academia on the nature of competition and the forces that drive the process. It was Porter who introduced the famous "5 Forces" model: the bargaining power of the supplier, the bargaining power of the customer, competition between existing players, the threat of new entrants and the threat of substitution, that has been used by many to explain how the competitive process has worked in particular industries. In *The Competitive Advantage of Nations* he turned his ideas and his attention to the global stage.

In this text he identified the fundamental determinants of national competitive advantage in an industry and how they work together to give international advantage. The findings had implications for firms and governments and set the agenda for discussions of global competition. The most relevant of his books for this material are listed below:

» Books: *Competitive Advantage* (1980).
  Cases in Competitive Strategy (1982).
  Competitive Strategy (1985).
  On Competition (1998).
  The Competitive Advantage of Nations (1998) (new revised edition).

Roos, Johan

Co-author of *Strategic Alliances* with Peter Lorange (see above), Johan Roos, assistant professor at the Norwegian School of Management, has written extensively on the subject of organizational knowledge and intellectual capital. Given that it is often expertise that is much sought after in acquisitions as well as assets, this is a growing area of research.

» Books: *Strategic Alliances* with Peter Lorange (1992).
  Managing Knowledge (ed.) with G. von Krogh (1996).
  Intellectual Common Sense (1997).
  Intellectual Capital (1997).

Tichy, Noel M.

Noel M. Tichy is a professor of organizational behavior and human resource management at the University of Michigan Business School, where he is the director of the Global Leadership Program and an authority on business growth.

Between 1985 and 1987, Tichy was responsible for management education at General Electric where he directed its worldwide management development programs. Prior to joining the Michigan Faculty he served for nine years on the Columbia University Business School Faculty.

Tichy is the author of numerous books and articles. Of especial interest in the context of this material is his 1998 book *Every Business Is a Growth Business* written in partnership with Ram Charan. In 1997 he co-authored *The Leadership Engine: How Winning Companies Build Leaders at Every Level* with Eli Cohen, named one of the top 10 business books of the year by *Business Week*. He is also the co-author with Stratford Sherman of *Control Your Destiny or Someone Else Will: How Jack Welch is Making General Electric the World's Most Competitive Company* and the author of both *Corporate Global Citizenship* and *Strategic Change Management* in addition to a number of texts on leadership and human resource management.

Tichy has served on the editorial boards of the *Academy of Management Review*, *Organizational Dynamics*, the *Journal of Business Research*, and the *Journal of Business Strategy*. He is past chairman of the Academy of Management's Organization and Management Theory Division and is a member of the board of governors of the American Society for Training and Development. He was the 1987 recipient of the New Perspectives on Executive Leadership Award by Johnson Smith & Knisely for the most outstanding contribution to the field as captured in *The Transformational Leader* written with Mary Anne Devanna. He received the 1993 Best Practice Award from the American Society for Training and Development and the 1994 Sales and Marketing Executives International Educator of the Year Award. Tichy is the founder and editor in chief of the *Human Resource Management Journal*.

Noel Tichy has been widely consulted by a variety of organizations. He is a senior partner in Action Learning Associates. His clients have included: Ameritech, AT&T, Mercedes-Benz, BellSouth, CIBA-GEIGY, Chase Manhattan Bank, Citibank, Exxon, General Electric, General Motors, Honeywell, Hitachi, Imperial Chemical Inc., IBM, NEC, Northern Telecom, Nomura Securities and 3M.

» Books: *Managing Strategic Change* (1983).

   Control Your Destiny or Someone Else Will: How Jack Welch is Making General Electric the World's Most Competitive Company with S. Sherman (1994).

Every Business Is a Growth Business with R. Charan (1997).
The Leadership Engine: How Winning Companies Build Leaders at Every Level (1997).
Corporate Global Citizenship (1997).
The Transformational Leader with M.A. Devanna (1997).

Weitzen, H. Skip

Weitzen, author of *Hypergrowth* (1991) was one of the earlier researchers to look at the phenomenon of hypergrowth. He drew the valid conclusions that hypergrowth depended upon giving the customer what they wanted, building a robust and flexible management team, developing a sound distribution and logistics network, partnerships, and creative financing. Weitzen is eminently readable and even after a decade his ideas are still highly applicable to fast growing companies. As mentioned in this material, Weitzen defined hypergrowth in terms of $1bn within a decade of growth beginning. That figure has probably increased somewhat since 1991 and thus his figures need to be considered relative to the time in which they were derived.

» Books: *Hypergrowth* (1991).

White, David

See Baghai, Mehrdad above.

» Books: *The Alchemy of Growth* with M. Baghai and S. Coley (1999).

Zook, Chris

As a director of Bain & Co, a global consultancy firm, Chris Zook (and his colleague James Allen) undertook a 10-year study of 2000 companies. They concluded that most growth and most profit came from core activities where the company could exploit its traditional expertise. In many ways this presents a counterpoint to the nonsynergical arguments of Anslinger and Copeland (above).

Zook does recognize the importance of what are termed "adjacent opportunities" for diversification, something that the Carnival

Corporation (Chapter 7) have proved adept at exploiting in its hyper-growth.

Profit from the Core is a useful starting point for anybody seeking information about the growth process.

» Books: *Profit from the Core* with J. Allen (2001).

Resources for Hypergrowth Strategies

This chapter identifies some of the best resources available for studying hypergrowth including:

- » general texts;
- » specific texts;
- » journals and magazines;
- » Websites.

Note: Dates of books in this chapter may differ from those shown in previous chapters. The dates here are of editions that have been revised from the date of first publication as shown in the chapter material.

Anslinger, P.L. and Copeland, T.E. (1994), "Growth Through Acquisitions", in *Strategies for Growth*, Harvard Business School, Cambridge, MA.

Baghai, M., Coley, S. and White, D. (1999), *The Alchemy of Growth*, Texere, London.

Cartwright, R. (2001), *Mastering Marketing Management*, Palgrave, Basingstoke.

Cartwright, R. and Green, G. (1997), *In Charge of Customer Satisfaction*, Blackwell, Oxford.

Copeland, T. (1988), *Financial Theory and Corporate Policy*, Addison Wesley, New York.

Dauphinais, W.G., Means, G.E., Price, C. and Gardner, G. (2000), *Wisdom of CEOs: Global Leaders Tackle Today's Most Pressing Challenges*, Wiley, New York.

Ellwood, W. (2001), *The No-nonsense Guide to Globalization*, New Internationalist, Oxford.

Heinecke, W.E. and Marsh, J. (2000), *The Entrepreneur: 21 Golden Rules for the Global Business Manager*, John Wiley & Sons (Asia), Singapore.

Hertz, N. (2001), *The Silent Takeover*, Heinemann, London.

Klein, N. (2000), *No Logo*, Flamingo, London.

Korten, D.C. (1996), *When Corporations Rule the World*, Berrett-Koehler, San Francisco.

Lorange, P. (1994), *The Strategic Planning Process*, Dartmouth, London.

Lorange, P. and Roos, J. (1992), *Strategic Alliances*, Blackwell, Cambridge, MA.

Means, G.E. and Schneider, D. (2000), *MetaCapitalism*, Wiley, New York.

Meyer, P. (2000), *Warp-Speed Growth*, Amacom, New York.

Mintzberg, H., Quinn, J.B. and James, R.M. (1988), *The Strategy Process*, Prentice Hall, Englewood Cliffs, NJ.

Peters, T. and Waterman, R. (1982), *In Search of Excellence*, Harper & Row, New York.

Porter, M. (1980), *Competitive Advantage*, Free Press, New York.

Porter, M. (1982), *Cases in Competitive Strategy*, Free Press, New York.

Porter, M. (1985), *Competitive Strategy*, Free Press, New York.

Porter, M. (1998), *On Competition*, Harvard Business School, Cambridge, MA.

Roos, J. (1997), *Intellectual Capital*, Palgrave/Macmillan, Basingstoke.

Roos, J. (1997), *Intellectual Common Sense*, Palgrave/Macmillan, Basingstoke.

Roos, J. and von Krogh, G. (eds) (1996), *Managing Knowledge*, Sage, London.

Tichy, N. (1983), *Managing Strategic Change*, Wiley, New York.

Tichy, N. (1997), *Corporate Global Citizenship*, Jossey Bass, San Francisco.

Tichy, N. (1997), *The Leadership Engine*, HarperCollins, New York.

Tichy, N. and Charan, R. (1998), *Every Business Is a Growth Business*, Random House, New York.

Tichy, N. and Devanna, M.A. (1997), *The Transformational Leader: The Key to Global Competitiveness*, Wiley, New York.

Tichy, N. and Sherman, S. (1994), *Control your Destiny or Somebody Else Will: How Jack Welch is Making General Electric the World's Most Competitive Company*, Harper Business, New York.

Weitzen, H. Skip (1991), *Hypergrowth: Applying the Success Formula of Today's Fastest Growing Companies*, Wiley, New York.

Zook, C. and Allen, J. (2001), *Profit from the Core*, Harvard Business School, Cambridge, MA.

For information about Airbus Industrie and the aircraft industry

Eddy, P., Potter, E. and Page, B. (1976), *Destination Disaster*, Hart–Davis, London.

Irving, C. (1993), *Wide Body, the Making of the Boeing 747*, Hodder & Stoughton, London.

Lynn, M. (1995), *Birds of Prey, Boeing v. Airbus*, Heinemann, London.

Sabbach, K. (1995), *21st Century Jet: The Making of the Boeing 777*, Macmillan, Basingstoke.

For information about amazon.com

Spector, R. (2000), *Amazon.com: Get Big Fast*, Random House, London.

For information about Carnival and the cruise industry

Cartwright, R. and Baird, C. (1999), *The Development and Growth of the Cruise Industry*, Butterworth-Heinemann, Oxford.

Dickinson, R. and Vladimir, A. (1997), *Selling the Sea*, Wiley, New York.

Ward, D. (2000), *The Berlitz Guide to Cruising and Cruise Ships 2001*, Berlitz, Princeton, NJ.

For information about Cisco Systems

Stauffer, D. (2000), *Business the Cisco Way*, Capstone, Oxford.

For information about culture

Lewis, R.D. (2000), *When Cultures Collide*, Nicholas Brealey, London.

Moran, R.T. and Harris, P.R. (2000), *Managing Cultural Differences*, Gulf Publishing Co., Houston.

Trompenaars, F. (1993), *Riding the Waves of Culture*, Economist Books, London.

For information about Hyundai and Samsung

Hiscock, G. (2000), *Asia's New Wealth Club*, Nicolas Brealey, London.

For information on the Internet, AOL and Internet-related growth

Aldrich, D.F. (1999), *Mastering the Digital Marketplace*, Wiley, New York.

Byrd, L. (2001), *Business the Oracle Way*, Capstone, Oxford.

Crainer, S. (2001), *Business the Jack Welch Way*, Capstone, Oxford.

Dearlove, D. (2001), *Business the Bill Gates Way*, Capstone, Oxford.

Dearlove, D. (2001), *Business the Richard Branson Way*, Capstone, Oxford.

Fortier, J. (2001), *Business the Sun Way*, Capstone, Oxford.
Merriden, T. (2001), *Business the Nokia Way*, Capstone, Oxford.
Price, C. (2000), *The Internet Entrepreneurs*, London, Pearson.
Saunders, R. (2000), *Business the Dell Way*, Capstone, Oxford.
Saunders, R. (2001), *Business the Amazon Way*, Capstone, Oxford.
Smith, R. and Vlamis, A. (2000), *Business the Yahoo! Way*, Capstone, Oxford.
Stauffer, D. (2000), *Business the AOL Way*, Capstone, Oxford.

For information on J P Morgan

Davie, M. (1986), *Titanic: The Full Story of a Tragedy*, Bodley Head, London.
Gardiner, R. and Van der Vat, D. (1995), *The Riddle of the Titanic*, Weidenfeld & Nicolson, London.
Strouse, J. (2000), *Morgan: An American Financier*, Harper Perennial, New York.

For information about Nike

Goldman, R. and Papson, S. (1999), *Nike Culture*, Sage, London.
Katz, D.R. (1995), *Just Do It – The Nike Spirit in the Corporate World*, Adams, New York.

MAGAZINES AND JOURNALS

Those interested in hypergrowth should consult the quality newspapers of the areas/countries they are interested in. Major Western broadsheet-type newspapers, e.g. the *Washington Post, New York Times, Herald Tribune, The Times, Daily Telegraph, Observer, Le Monde* etc., provide useful analysis of news and financial/business matters and cover international in addition to national news. Current affairs and other relevant programs on the radio or television are useful but, as with newspapers, a translator may be required. Most major newspapers now have an online edition.

The following, most of which are published online as well as in hard copy (see Websites at the end of this chapter), are useful sources of information about markets, competitors, and developments. The

Websites should be accessed for subscription rates, samples and special subscription offers.

Business 2.0

Business and financial daily carrying articles etc. of an international nature. The importance of scanning such material for items of possible interest cannot be overstated as most hypergrowth companies are global in nature, a knowledge of world affairs is vital to management of such concerns.

Economist

Weekly current affairs magazine with a global approach and thus very useful. The *Economist* carries general current affairs news in addition to analysis and market news on a global basis. Issued both as a print version and online. Available by subscription or from news-stands.

Forbes

Forbes is leading company providing resources for the world's business and investment leaders, providing them with commentary, analysis, relevant tools and real-time reporting; includes real-time original reporting on business, technology, investing and lifestyle. *Forbes* is extremely useful reading for all those involved with expanding business.

The weekly *Forbes* magazine is also available online and while mainly designed for a US audience is read on a global basis. *Forbes* often carries articles and commentaries on growth issues. Other linked products from Forbes include:

» *Forbes Global*: covering the rise of capitalism around the world for international business leaders. Contains sections on companies and industry, capital markets and investing, entrepreneurs, technology and *Forbes Global Life*.
» Forbes Newsletters including:
  Forbes Aggressive Growth Investor, a monthly newsletter recommending the 50 best growth and momentum stocks to own now as determined by a proprietary multi-dimensional computer analysis of over 3000 stocks.

Gilder Technology Report covering the smartest, most profitable way to invest in technology.

Special Situation Survey with monthly stock recommendations, hold or sell advice on each recommendation and special investment reports – tends to be of interest mainly to investors in the US, of which there are many in Europe and Asia.

New Economy Watch: a newsletter that looks at Internet-based companies.

Harvard Business Review

This is a leading business and management resource that is read worldwide and features contributions by the leading names in business and management. It is published 10 times a year and available by subscription. Many of the world's leading authorities on growth and its effects have been published in the *Harvard Business Review* and it should be one of the journals that is available to managers throughout the world, so influential are those contributing to it.

McKinsey Quarterly

This material has featured a number of members of McKinsey & Company. Each quarter the company publishes an authoritative online journal that contains features and articles, many of which are associated with business growth.

PricewaterhouseCoopers

The consulting firm of PricewaterhouseCoopers produces a series of publications including the *Management, Trendsetter*, and *Technology Barometers*, details of which are contained on their Website. The *Trendsetter Barometer*, for example, is a quarterly telephone survey of more than 400 CEOs of rapid/hypergrowth companies and is therefore useful in predicting trends etc. The companies forming the survey all have growth rates of at least 25 percent per annum.

Sloan Management Review

The management journal of MIT (Massachusetts's Institute of Technology), this journal attracts some of the world's leading authorities on business and management. Growth and associated issues are a frequent feature of the articles. The range of the journal is global and not confined to the US. The *Sloan Management Review* is published quarterly.

Sun Microsystems

Sun Microsystems provide advice and seminars of especial use to potential dot-com companies. The Sun Startup Program is of especial use to Internet entrepreneurs. The company also provides a list of useful business reading that is not confined to technology but is also linked to all aspects of business. Details can be found on the company Website.

Time

Time magazine, while originally a US product, has a global readership and is one of the most important current affairs and commentary magazines in existence. To appear on the cover of *Time* is to have made it; to be the *Time* man/woman of the year is a considerable honor indeed. Many of the personalities featured have been associated with hypergrowth.

Time covers a huge range of issues and is thus a useful tool for those involved in global expansion. The print version is available either on subscription or from news-stands.

Time was the first news magazine to publish online, beginning in 1993 and launched TIME.com in 1994. According to Nielsen NetRatings, TIME.com is the most trafficked news magazine site online. TIME.com draws over 5 million visits per month and receives over 32 million monthly page views. The site covers the events impacting the world each day and offers its own perspective on the latest news. There are also sections entitled Nation, Education, World, and Health.

Wall Street Journal

This is a US financial daily carrying analysis, financial and other commercial news plus company results. Available on subscription or from news-stands.

TRADE AND PROFESSIONAL JOURNALS

Each company operates in its own sectors and particular marketplace with a set of product, services or ideas unique to the sector to at least some extent.

In addition to understanding the general world of business and commerce there will be specific sectoral requirements and knowledge that the company needs to consider when contemplating growth. This is especially important when looking at companies in other sectors that may be being considered for an acquisition.

WEBSITES

» www.airbus.com – Airbus Industrie Website
» www.amazon.com – Amazon.com Website
» www.barometersurveys.com – Barometer Surveys Website
» www.business2.com – Business 2 Website
» www.carnivalcorp.com – Carnival Website
» www.cisco.com – Cisco Systems Website
» www.economist.com – Economist Website
» www.forbes.com – Forbes Website
» www.hbsp.harvard.edu/products/hbr – Harvard Business Review Website
» www.mckinseyquarterly.com – McKinsey Quarterly Website
» www.nike.com – Nike Website
» www.mitsloan.mit.edu – Sloan Management Review Website
» www.pwcglobal.com – PricewaterhouseCoopers Website
» www.samsung.com – Samsung Website
» www.sun.com – Sun Microsystems Website

Ten Steps to Hypergrowth

This final chapter provides some key insights into managing hyper-growth, covering the following steps:

- » know the customer;
- » understand the market;
- » sort out the money;
- » be at the cutting edge;
- » control costs;
- » remember the value chain;
- » be the best;
- » forge alliances;
- » have and communicate a vision;
- » control the growth.

The steps below are designed to assist you in understanding what actions need to be taken to stimulate and sustain hypergrowth. There are no guarantees that hypergrowth will occur but without these steps it is highly unlikely to do so.

1. KNOW THE CUSTOMER

Hypergrowth companies spend a considerable time getting to know their customers. Wherever they may be operating, time is spent before entering a market to ensure that the products and services to be offered correspond to the needs and wants of the potential customer base. Hypergrowth companies realize that they have not only to grow their operation but their customer base. They do this by being customer, rather than product, centered.

Whenever one hears of companies beginning to behave in an arrogant or disdainful manner to their customers (this is often the main subject of TV consumer programs) it is a sure sign that the hypergrowth phase is over and the organization is beginning to atrophy. Management should take very careful note of customer comments. Once customers feel that they are no longer special they will take their business elsewhere.

2. UNDERSTAND THE MARKET

Markets are complex manifestations of the trading process. They comprise not only buyers and sellers but also those who support the transaction process. Unless a company has an excellent understanding of what the market wants and how it will behave, hypergrowth is virtually impossible to sustain. The understanding should extend to the competition – they will not be standing still while another company expands. They will want their share of the action. Understanding the competition and understanding one's own value chain are as important as understanding the customer as described in Step 1.

3. SORT OUT THE MONEY

Money, it is said, "makes the world go around." Growth requires financial resources and hypergrowth may require very large amounts initially to pump, prime, and start the process. Once hypergrowth is underway, revenues should come on stream. While it may well be necessary to pay part of the profits as dividends, some should be used to reward staff for their part in the hypergrowth process and some re-invested to fund even more growth. Remember, plant and equipment wear out and will need replacing.

If the hypergrowth produces large cash reserves, then the company can look at funding even more growth through acquisitions.

Joint ventures are a useful method of sharing the financial burden of projects and may well ease a company into a new market or area of activity on the back of their partner's expertise and resources.

Cashflow is all-important. A company should never run out of cash. To do so is to become extremely vulnerable to a cash rich predator and to risk loss of independence.

4. BE AT THE CUTTING EDGE

Hypergrowth companies are at the cutting edge of what they do. They lead developments. Hypergrowth is rarely achieved by those companies that are followers – sometimes referred to as ''me too'' companies.

If the company does not have the development expertise, it often buys it in – not just by outsourcing but by purchasing a smaller, developmental operation. This can be beneficial to all concerned as such small operations can then use the financial resources and buying power of the larger one.

It is not just in technological developments that there is a cutting edge – the means of retailing, new markets, new production methods etc. are all features of hypergrowth operations. These are companies that are constantly ''pushing the envelope'' and doing things in different ways. In this way they gain extra publicity by being noticed and commented on more frequently than their competitors.

5. CONTROL COSTS

Hypergrowth can be a very exciting time but in the frenzy the need to control costs can be forgotten. Hypergrowth is not just about larger companies and more output – if the inputs cost more than the outputs, the company is in trouble.

Hypergrowth companies should have hard-headed financial control staff in place to seek the best deals from suppliers etc. Companies that fail to control costs are the ones that run into cashflow problems (see Step 3). If it can be done at a lower cost without compromising quality then it should be.

6. REMEMBER THE VALUE CHAIN

No organization can carry out its tasks independently of others. Suppliers form an important part of the chain that adds value – value that is eventually translated into profit.

Hypergrowth companies depend on receiving a constant supply of materials. Their growth can assist growth for their suppliers, although they need to take care that they do not become too dependent upon single sources of supply. If this happens any glitch in the supply/value chain can easily be translated into a problem for the customer – the ultimate link in the chain.

Many companies supply training and support to their prime suppliers so that they are aware of what is happening and can play a full part in any developments. It can be all to easy for a company that is growing at a fast rate to believe that it is doing it all by itself, but the truth is that hypergrowth depends on a large number of people and even organizations working together for mutual benefit.

7. BE THE BEST

Quality at a reasonable price is something that appeals to all customers. Hypergrowth companies are consistently among the best in their chosen fields and markets. Quality actually comes with little ultimate cost. The cost of not doing something properly whether it be the cost of rectification or the cost of losing a customer is nearly always greater than the cost of delivering a quality product or service. Hypergrowth companies know this and offer high quality and value for money.

By the late twentieth and the early twenty-first centuries the concept of zero-defect products had become an achievable reality and something that consumers expect as of right. The time and resource spent on making sure of quality is never wasted. Without the foundation of quality, value for money products and services hypergrowth is an unattainable dream.

8. FORGE ALLIANCES

Entering new markets or new fields of operation can be exceptionally expensive and time consuming. It makes sense, therefore, for companies to ally themselves with those possessing the necessary expertise. This may be through acquisition but if it does not prejudice the company in a competitive sense then an alliance may be a suitable option.

Alliances may be for just a single project or they may lead to merger and acquisition. They provide a useful method for testing out markets and relationships. Many of the products of the current automobile industry are produced through alliances of design and manufacturing with the partners selling what are basically similar products under their own brand names and marketing networks.

9. HAVE AND COMMUNICATE A VISION

Without vision and a knowledge of where the company is going, growth and especially any hypergrowth will be unfocussed and ephemeral. The vision should not just be held by senior management but needs to be communicated throughout the company and along the value chain so that everybody can understand the part they will have to play in making it a reality.

10. CONTROL THE GROWTH

Hypergrowth is highly exciting but needs to be controlled. The dangers of running out of resources and especially cash have already been stressed in this material. Hypergrowth companies keep a tight rein on the resources to ensure that the growth does not become so chaotic as to threaten the company itself.

Having a vision and a picture of the way forward helps to ensure that developments are in line with the desired progress.

There may well be times when potential growth has to be declined as it does not fit in with the vision and may divert attention away from the other activities of the company. Hypergrowth, when it is controlled, is exciting and fun; uncontrolled the excitement can soon change to panic.

KEY LEARNING POINTS

Hypergrowth does not just happen, it comes about because a company:

- » has a vision and a mission;
- » knows where it wants to go;
- » is able to control growth and costs;
- » keeps a close eye on its cash;
- » works with others where necessary;
- » values all members of the value chain; and
- » has listened to its customers.

Frequently Asked Questions (FAQs)

Q1: Is hypergrowth only seen in large companies?

A: All companies start small. Hypergrowth is rapid growth relative to others in the same area of operation. Hypergrowth that produces revenues of $1bn in a short time may be only for the few but hypergrowth relative to competitors is always possible for the company that offers its customers exactly what they require. The larger a company the more it can demand discounts on its supplies, thus cutting costs. See Chapters 1, 2 and 6 for more details.

Q2: Does hypergrowth need large cash reserves to support it?

A: In any commercial operation there is normally a time lag between development expenditure and the revenue stream coming online. This gap has to be plugged using either cash reserves or borrowed money. Very rapid growth may well need additional cash resources to fund it. Careful market analysis is needed to ensure that the revenues will cover any repayments. There is more about this in Chapter 6.

Q3: Can everybody in a market achieve hypergrowth simultaneously?

A: It is certainly possible for a whole market to achieve hypergrowth. The jet airliner market in the 1950s, the color TV market as soon as color sets were available, and the cruise market (see Chapter 7) have all shown hypergrowth in recent years. Not every company has benefited – some have been unable to cope and have either gone out of business entirely or have been acquired by the more successful. See Chapters 6 and 7 for more details.

Q4: How can the Internet and e-commerce assist and stimulate hypergrowth?

A: All companies can benefit from the increased access to customers that the Internet and e-commerce can bring them. Additionally Internet usage is itself in hypergrowth, bringing tremendous growth opportunities to those companies that support Internet services. The role of the Internet and e-commerce is the subject of Chapter 4.

Q5: Does hypergrowth always involve global expansion?

A: Unless a company is located in one of the very large countries of the world, hypergrowth often means that it needs to seek customers outwith its own locality. Many companies grow by moving first to adjacent countries and then further afield. Joint ventures and alliances can make this easier to accomplish and lessen the risks. The global implications of hypergrowth are covered in Chapter 5.

Q6: What advantages does hypergrowth provide for a company?

A: In addition to larger companies being able to use economies of scale in acquiring resources, growth and success often bred further growth and success. The names of hypergrowth companies are often household names, thus providing a form of free advertising. Increased profits please the investors and make others even more willing to invest and this can drive the share price up thus increasing the value of the company. Hypergrowth also provides the company with considerable bargaining power with governments etc. It is probably a truism in today's commercial world that it is either better to be big and still growing or small. It is often the middle-sized, stagnant companies that are squeezed in highly competitive markets. You can read more about this in Chapters 1, 2 and 6.

Q7: How important are acquisitions to hypergrowth?

A: Acquisitions, often of rivals or companies in the adolescent phase of their life cycle are one of the main methods used by rapidly growing companies. In this way they acquire expertise and the all-important customer base. See Chapters 2, 6 and 7 for details and examples.

Q8: Is hypergrowth just a recent phenomenon?

A: In terms of the huge sums of money involved, writers such as Weitzen believe that it started in the 1980s. However, there have been organizations that have grown with exceeding rapidity relative to others throughout history and certainly since the Industrial Revolution. Shipbuilding, railways, electronics have all exhibited hypergrowth in the past. Chapter 3 provides a history of hypergrowth.

Q9: Can hypergrowth go on forever?

A: Nothing lasts forever. Growth usually slows down but as the rejuvenation phase of the organizational life cycle shows, it is possible to have a period of stability and to follow that by more growth. If the company has a history of hypergrowth in the past it may be more likely to stimulate and sustain hypergrowth again in the future. See Chapter 2 for the organizational life cycle.

Q10: Where are resources available to assist in understanding strategies for hypergrowth?

A: A list of books, journals and Web addresses can be found in Chapter 9.

Index

Printed and bound in the UK by
CPI Antony Rowe, Eastbourne

Printed and bound by CPI Group (UK) Ltd, Croydon, CR0 4YY

13/04/2025

14656558-0001